The Book of the LNER Pacifics
Modelling Options

By Tony Wright

Assistant Editor British Railway Modelling

Published by
Irwell Press

Copyright IRWELL PRESS LIMITED
ISBN 978-1-906919-16-0
First published in the United Kingdom in 2010
by Irwell Press Limited, 59A, High Street, Clophill,
Bedfordshire MK45 4BE
Printed by Konway Press

A NOTE

As touched on in the Introduction, it is not the intention to give a full history of all those models representing the LNER 4-6-2s; instead there is a brief overview at the start of each chapter, before considering some of the modelling options. For any omissions I must offer apologies beforehand, especially to any manufacturers whose work is not present. My photographic collection won't cover every single item, and if a 'historic' picture has been used before in another publication, I hope readers will forgive me, for it 'completes' the story so to speak. This account is designed to complement the Irwell Press 'Book Of' series (in this case obviously the principal LNER Pacifics) which now covers most of our main and many of our not so main line classes, both diesel and steam. If it proves popular, then maybe other *Modelling Options* will follow – even the Pannier Tanks!

Dedication

This book is warmly dedicated to Simon Kohler of Hornby and Graham Hubbard of Bachmann for at last giving us brilliant, ready-to-run examples of Gresley's and Peppercorn's Pacifics.

Contents

A magnificent collection of Eastern Region RA9 motive power, 'posed' for the camera in typical publicity department guise (yes, I know there's a V2 as well, but that's just as much a part of the 'Big-Engine' policy as any 4-6-2). The line up is on John Ryan's Over Peover in O gauge, and all these locomotives have been professionally built from DJH kits in O gauge.

4

The Book of the LNER Pacifics
Modelling Options
INTRODUCTION

The idea for this book came out of a chance conversation with Chris Hawkins of Irwell Press, where he asked me if (of all things!) I might have enough photographic material to illustrate a 'modelling options' book on the GWR Pannier tanks. I said I'd look through my collection, but it would be unlikely that there'd be much, assuming I could remember where all the images might be. You see, although I class myself as a railway/model railway enthusiast, I don't have a particular interest or knowledge regarding the GWR or the Western Region (even though I saw operations on the latter just about every day as a trainspotter in my native Chester). And, though I've probably taken hundreds of model railway pictures featuring GWR/WR motive power, it would have required considerable time for me to sort through those images, even assuming I could remember where they all were. I then suggested that it's a pity Irwell isn't considering doing a modelling options book on the LNER/ER RA9 stuff, and that's how this book came about!

I know it's obvious propaganda, but the three Irwell 'Books Of' written by Peter Coster describing the LNER Pacifics are now regarded by enthusiasts as the definitive works on the subject. True, they are complementary to the volumes produced by the RCTS and Willie Yeadon but neither of those cover the subject in such a comprehensive way or contain fewer mistakes. In fact, despite hours spent on dissecting Peter's work, other than the (very rare) error in describing a location, they are just about mistake-free. As such, they are invaluable to the historian and model maker. And it's the latter where I think I come in.

For the last 40 years, I've built models of Eastern Region locomotives and rolling stock for myself. I've also built models representing other railways in my 14 years (1990-2003) as a professional model maker but they were for customers. During those professional years I also built dozens of models of what's represented in this book for customers (they were hard to let go of at times!), for that was my area of

specialism. Why? As is probably well known by now, my principal interest in both the hobbies of railway enthusiasm and model railway enthusiasm is the Eastern Region of British Railways, mainly the East Coast Main Line. Though a North Westerner by birth, paternal relations in the West Riding ensured I had a regular base from which to watch my favourites. Being an immediate post-war 'baby boomer' meant my trainspotting years were the mid-'50s to the early-'60s, surely one of the most interesting times on our home railways. Thus, when I started, steam still held the upper hand and as I finished, diesels and electrics were in the ascendancy. My first efforts at making models were pretty grotty. Lack of experience, dodgy kits and an extremely limited (and poor in terms of accuracy) ready-to-run base meant success was never going to be easy. Some of those earlier efforts are included in this book, though only for comparative purposes for, I hope, the modelling options I consider should achieve excellence. And they do in most

The exceptional current standards now offered by the likes of Hornby in RTR OO are no better illustrated here than in this out-of-the-box model of *Great Northern* in her first LNER manifestation. She is in original A1 condition (other than losing her GNR identity) with tall cab and boiler fittings, open front footsteps, completely rectangular buffer beam, short travel valves (note the lack of a thin 'box' around the base of the outside steampipes) and number on tender. The exquisite paint job is fully up to professional standards (indeed, beyond some practitioners) and it's parked on the turntable of Top Shed on Cliff Parson's Gresley Beat layout.

cases, for what follows should be a celebration of the wonderful models one can now obtain or achieve of the LNER Pacifics. That this is principally down to the work/products of others is no surprise.

I count it an immense privilege to have been able to earn a living since 1990 from making models, photographing them and writing about them. And not just my own models,

but photographing hundreds (perhaps even over a thousand by now) of model railways, all over the country, in my capacity as a free-lance photographer, working for all the model railway magazines. Since 2003, when I was appointed Assistant Editor/Photographer, my photography and writing have been confined to one magazine, *British Railway Modelling*, published by Warners Group

Publications. Thus, all the model pictures in this volume are: *by courtesy BRM, Warners Group Publications*. My publisher, John Greenwood, is enlightened enough to let me write this book on a free-lance basis and I hope the link between Warners and Irwell is seen as being complementary and that this volume exploits the link between Irwell's considerable expertise in prototype railway imagery and history

60042 *Singapore* on shed at Aberdeen Ferryhill, 14 September 1963. Like 60036 she has had the top lamp bracket lowered, with the consequent division of the smokebox door handrail. Part of the AWS equipment is just visible behind the protective plate.

Pacifics, there is such a wealth of published material that it is hard to recommend any particular book. RTCS *Locomotives of the LNER Part 2A* is almost a 'Bible' and is most valuable, while P. N. Townend's *East Coast Pacifics at Work* (Ian Allan) is also very useful.

To commence the conversion, remove the locomotive body from the chassis, taking care to screw the retaining bolt back into the body. Then remove the moulded ejector pipe, which runs along the right hand side of the boiler from the cab. I did this with a chisel-type craft knife blade. If you are careful, you can retain the boiler bands where they intersect the pipe. Gently rub down the boiler with fine wet-and-dry to make good.

If you are modelling an A3 without German-style deflectors, carefully remove the smokebox pipe joint and retain for use on the left hand side.

The new ejector pipe is fashioned from a 117mm length of 0.50mm diameter micro-rod, held in place with small split pins. Drill four holes in the appropriate positions on the boiler (consult photographs).

The pipe centreline should be approximately 24mm from the running plate at the firebox end, and 15mm from the exhaust passage casings mounted on the running plate at the smokebox end.

Once the ejector pipe has been fitted, carefully cut the reversing rod from below the right hand running plate. This will have to be located on the left hand side, albeit back to front. In view of the delicate nature of this item, I find it prudent to fit it out of sequence, almost at the end of the conversion.

It is worth pointing out here, in case you should choose one of the locomotives built by the North British Locomotive Company, that they fitted a different pattern of reversing rod, some of which survived until withdrawal. Once again, consult a good photograph.

Superheater header covers need to be fitted at the rear of the smokebox. Drill a hole 10mm

60059 *Tracery* leaving King's Cross, 16 October 1961. The outline of the Witte smoke deflectors can be clearly seen.

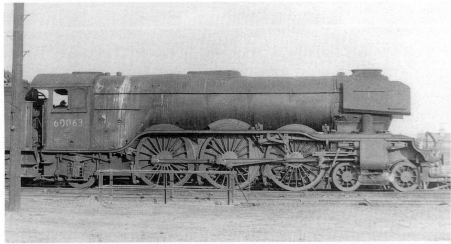

Six months from withdrawal, grimy 60063 *Isinglass* rests at Peterborough New England shed, 8 December 1963. Quite a contrast to the photograph above!

from the boiler centreline and 5mm from the leading boiler band. You will find that this will need to be opened out to allow the casings, available from King's Cross Models, to be fitted.

Whether you are modelling a single or double chimney engine, I feel it is best to remove the moulded chimney. It is, in my opinion, one of the least satisfactory aspects of the model as bought.

When removing this fitting, take care not to slice off the snifting valve, immediately behind the chimney.

The chimney may be replaced by either a cast double fitment, such as that made by Craftsman, or the beautiful turned brass single chimney available from W&H.

With regard to the dome, at the end of their lives nearly all carried the famous 'banjo' dome, though some, 60065/9/91/104 for instance, had the round dome (similar to that on the model as bought) fitted to boilers built by Thompson. If you fit a 'banjo', it should sit 10mm from the fourth boiler band from the smokebox, and in that case you will have to make good part of the third boiler band from the smokebox, with micro-strip or similar. You will find that once you have done this it will probably be necessary to blend in the new piece of boiler band by gently rubbing down with fine wet and dry paper.

Before leaving the subject of domes, it is as well to mention that the 'banjo' dome fitted to both the A3s and V2s, and to the post-war Pacifics, was of an almost 'tear drop' pattern. I believe that MJT Scale Components make such a casting. The more commonly available Craftsman casting is, I understand, of a pre-war design, with a noticeable waist.

During the course of their lives, some A3s were fitted with A4-type boilers (diagram 107). Engines so fitted are noticeable by the different placement of washout plugs on the firebox, together with a slight horizontal ridge where the firebox joins the boiler. Also note that the 'banjo' dome on these boilers is slightly further forward.

I have modified some of my engines in this fashion, though I must admit to being not totally convinced that this operation is worth the effort.

Turning to the cab, the most obvious variation is that during the 1930s the cab side sheets were raised, ie. the depth of the cutaway just behind the rear cab window was reduced.

I modified the cab cutaway by glueing two pieces of 10 thou plasticard shown in Fig. 1 to the inside of the cab. They should be so fitted to be 5mm above the existing cutaway. Before fitment, file a tight radius on the rear edge of the plasticard (see drawing).

60069 *Sceptre* at Dumfries with the Up *Thames-Clyde Express*, 24 May 1961. Note the Thompson boiler and round dome.

Once set, knead some Milliput or similar filler onto the plasticard, not forgetting to work a slight radius into the filler where it joins the rear cab pillar. Before the filler sets, it's best to make a pilot hole for the handrail knob, to be drilled when firm. Do not forget to fashion the beading round the outside edge of the new work. I used a small piece of filler finely rolled.

The new cutaway is probably the most time-consuming aspect of the conversion, but I feel it's well worth the effort.

For some reason, Hornby have chosen not to glaze the cab on this model. I cannot really understand why, since the 'Scotsman' must surely be considered to be one of the flagships of the Hornby stud.

I am not aware if South Eastern Models have extended their excellent range of flush glazing kits to include the A1; if not, no doubt they will.

I glazed the engine with clear plastic sheet. Flush glazing is not as difficult as it sounds. Cut two rectangles approx. 6mm by just under 8mm and carefully file to shape. Keep offering up the glazing to the window opening until you have a good fit. There's no hard-and-fast way of doing this, the process being a matter of trial and error.

The front spectacles are a somewhat easier proposition. Place the glazing material over a suitable drawing, mark out then cut and file to shape. I believe the spectacles as moulded by Hornby are slightly underscale, but if this is so it works in our favour since the front windows stand proud of the spectacle plate and can

be carefully glued in place onto the cab front itself.

One point regarding cab ventilators, 60066 had a cab with a high ventilator. It was transferred from (60)112 in January 1948.

One aspect of the A3 cab I decided not to portray was the turn-in of the rear sidesheets. However, I believe this to be possible should one desire this feature.

Turning our attention to the front end of the locomotive, a cover for the inside cylinder valve gear should be fitted. This is easily achieved by glueing two lengths of 20 × 20 thou micro-strip 17mm long between the frame ends above the buffer beam. These strips should be placed above and below the small detail which represents the middle cylinder just to the right of the left hand frame end. Once the 'runners' are firmly in place the 'cover' can be fitted. This is a piece of 10 thou plasticard 8mm × 3mm.

Whilst in the area of the buffer beam, there are a number of details to be added here.

Lamp irons are easily represented by drilling appropriately spaced holes immediately behind the buffer beam and then glueing a cut-down No. 56 staple in the hole. The 'upright' of the staple should point towards the cab and about 2mm of the 'crossbar' should project through the hole. Incidentally, since most of my A3s work express passenger trains, I usually fit only a centre lamp iron, merely glueing a lamp either side.

Turning to the top iron, I leave the moulded one in place, unless modelling an engine which received a lowered iron and split front handrail. These changes were effected from early 1962 on some A3s, V2s and post-war Pacifics. I understand that this amendment was brought about because if an engine was carrying a headboard in the top position, smoke would gather behind the board and the driver's vision would be impaired.

Should you need to fabricate a new top lamp iron, simply fold and crimp a No. 56 staple as shown in Fig. 2.

You may wish to fit spring buffers, in which case cut off the existing buffers and open out the resulting hole to accept the new buffers. Personally, I retain the Hornby buffers.

Those engines fitted with AWS (ie. all except Carlisle Canal Depot-based locomotives) were equipped with a plate directly behind the front coupling. This was designed to protect the AWS receiver. To represent this, cut a thin piece of brass sheet as shown in Fig. 3, then fold as shown in Fig. 4.

It's best to fit the screw link coupling before

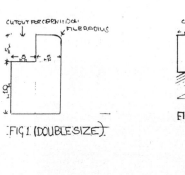

FIG 1. (DOUBLE SIZE)

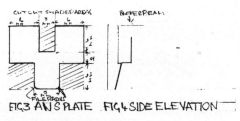

FIG 3 AWS PLATE   FIG 4 SIDE ELEVATION

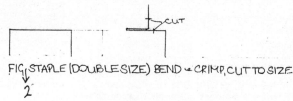

FIG STAPLE (DOUBLE SIZE) BEND & CRIMP, CUT TO SIZE

PLATFORM 1 BREAK INDICATED BY MILK CHURN

PLATFORM 2 BREAK INDICATED BY LINE BETWEEN POST BETWEEN TRACKS AND PORTER ON PLATFORM

CARRIAGE SIDING BREAK INDICATED BY POST

PLATFORM 3 BREAK INDICATED BY MILK CHURN

Section breaks
Thoughts for accurate operation
by Richard Kirkby

Photographs by Frank Green

CAN YOU see a rail joint when you are ten feet away or more? The reason I ask this question is that I cannot now do so. I might have been able to some years ago but I now need a guide which is more visible to tell me where a particular rail break is.

As soon as our two-rail layouts become even ever so slightly more complicated than a simple circuit we start to need dead sections of track in order to isolate motive power units from the otherwise ever-present electrical supply. We may need these isolating sections for a whole variety of reasons; to park individual locomotives in an engine shed (without everything else moving); to back a pilot locomotive onto a train already headed by another engine: to attach a shunting engine onto the rear of a train in order to pull out the roll-

ing stock from a siding or platform and thus release the train engine — and so on.

The 'isolating' or 'dead' section of track is the easiest electrical circuit. Two wires, one from each side of a rail gap, are led to a simple on/off switch. Some folk prefer a press-to-make button but as I always forget, at the critical moment, whether I have or have not pressed the button. I prefer a good, old-fashioned switch which shows at a glance whether power is on or off.

However, the problem remains of identifying where the gap is in order that we can carry out our operations satisfactory.

Here are a few of my 'long distance' solutions which enable me to judge (not see) when something is on an isolated piece of track:

a. a signal (main line or shunting) abreast the

rail break;
b. a gradient post, tree, telegraph pole in line between the operating position and the break;
c. a post, an end of some fencing, or the end of a building;
d. a milk churn — or other piece of platform 'furniture' including a designated passenger, guard etc;
e. a pile of sleepers between or alongside the track.

The list is endless and drawn from all the bits and pieces which surround the railway scene and make it look authentic. We clothe our layouts with such oddments to make it look right; my idea has been to use some of this impedimenta as a guide to accurate opering.

Five-inch extension for 'Maidenhaiste'

Continued from previous page

The shelving, and the table on the top floor, are mde from brass tube and sheet soldered up, and painted a dark green. The boxes on the shelves on the top floor, and the books on the shelves in the office downstairs, are made from brown envelopes which have been folded and Evostuck together. The interior is lit using grain-of-wheat bulbs, which should be masked when using spray paints otherwise you need to scrape all the paint off the glass. Unfortunately this is exactly what we had to do.

Having built the shed and obtained an MTK trolley the new 'longer' Maidenhaiste is doing the exhibition circuit, and giving pleasure to many.

The man with the drum on the coaling stage marks the section break on the coaling road. The rear of the ground signal (just to the left of the Schools Class) marks the break on the loco spur. Section switches visible behind false water tank.

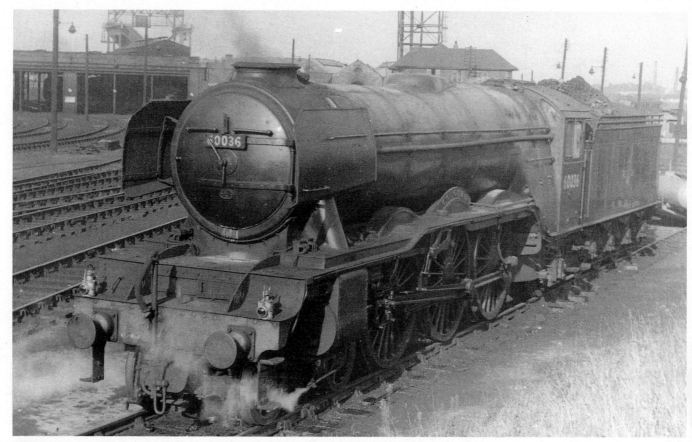

60036 *Colombo* at Darlington, 30 October 1964 in her penultimate month of service. Points to note are the lowered top lamp bracket, rear driver speedometer cable and AWS plate below bufferbeam. A GNR-type tender with coal rails is attached.

Gresley A1 to latter-day A3

A 4mm scale conversion for the Hornby Pacific

by Tom Burns

Prototype photographs: R. F. Orpwood, Gresley Society

Model photographs: Dave Brennand

THE GRESLEY A3s are to my mind one of the most beautiful locomotive classes ever, combining Edwardian elegance with a modern, powerful line.

In model form, they have long been favourites with manufacturers and modellers alike. In 16.5mm gauge there have been A3s from Trix

A3s at the Cross, 22 July 1961. All three (60112/061/048) have smoke deflecting fins atop smokebox. Chimney of 60078 visible behind that of *Pretty Polly*.

Twin (AC), Trix/Liliput (DC), Triang, Wills, Jameson, DJH and now Pro-scale. I always felt that the Triang model never did the prototype justice, somehow failing to capture the character of the graceful A3. Perhaps they felt the same way down at Margate since some years ago now they introduced a completely new model, in-

corporating their well-tried tender drive and a new body moulding.

The new model was certainly an improvement, though rather surprisingly, Hornby decided to portray the earlier A1 class. However, the new model was excellent and a good basis for conversion to an A3.

I model the 1958-62 period and therefore my locomotives are running at the close of their lives. There is a considerable amount of work entailed in this conversion, as follows:

Locomotive

Replacement of boiler mountings.
Conversion from right to left hand drive.
Alteration of middle cylinder cover.
Amendment of cab cutaway.
Replacement of moulded handrails, fitting of lamp irons.
Fitting of cylinder drain cocks.

Tender

The tender as supplied with the model represents an original 1928 corridor tender and as such is not suitable for any BR A3, or indeed LNER A3, after August 1937. Therefore, a completely new tender body has to be substituted.

The conversion

As with all such conversions, it is wise to arm yourself with appropriate books, photographs and drawings. When it comes to the Gresley

Chapter 1
GRESLEY A1

Traditionally this type has not been well covered in model form, though things are getting better. Hornby's current OO RTR example is magnificent (their earlier, tender-drive examples are not so good) and there are some excellent kits, particularly in O gauge from the likes of DJH and Martin Finney. With work, DJH and South Eastern Finecast A3 kits can be altered to become A1s, and Jamieson's A3 kit was actually nearer to an A1 than the improved successor. For the collector, Bassett Lowke made an A1 pre and post-war.

Two superb views of *Great Northern*, the top one showing her in original GNR condition. In the lower shot, she's now the LNER's property with 'nibbles' out of her bufferbeam but still with tall fittings.

From the sublime... as the saying goes, and here is a pair of Bassett Lowke A1s in (very) coarse scale. Both represent *Flying Scotsman* and show the loco in pre-war and post-war condition. This list of 'inaccuracies' is enormous though par for the course for obsolete tinplate. Assuming there's an indication of a drive side then it's on the wrong side (at least for the LNER version – where's the vacuum ejector pipe?). Both tow corridor tenders (only correct for earlier LNER days and NEVER in BR days) and when 60103 became BR's property (certainly when it was green) it was an A3 (superheater header covers on smokebox sides). Since Bassett Lowke had no thought for such minutiae of realism and collectors of this stuff don't give two hoots, I only include them for historical interest, since no 'serious' railway modeller would use them (though Jack Ray of Crewchester fame made a most convincing model out of one, thus ruining its value!). However, it's a salutary thought to consider that these 'gross' and inaccurate models are worth more than Steve Barnfield's masterpieces! It's also an interesting thought that some of the errors mentioned were cheerfully perpetuated years later in OO gauge, of which more later.

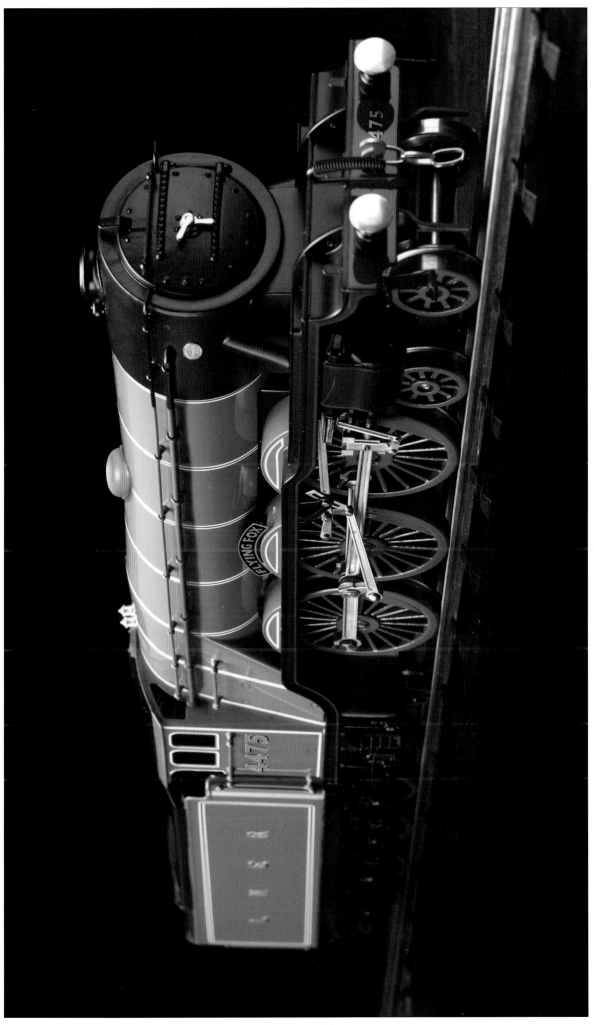

Current Bassett Lowke (now under Hornby's wing) and much less coarse scale gauge O. This A1 actually has a drive side (correctly right-hand, though there's no reversing lever). Its side handrails also turn in at the front to be clipped to the smokebox ring. It has lower fittings, long travel valves and tows a corridor tender, making this manifestation of *Flying Fox* correct for the late-'20s/ mid-'30s. Now made in the Far East (rather than Germany), these models perpetuate the Bassett Lowke collectors' theme, though they're much cheaper than the old ones, even though they're more accurate.

Current ready-to-run excellence in gauge O as shown by this Sunset Models A1, representing *Flying Scotsman* in late-'20s/mid-'30s condition. Substantially accurate and beautifully finished, the cost is probably a bit more than twice as much as the current Bassett Lowke item, though it's infinitely more realistic. There are a few issues – the 1928 corridor tender has no beading on this sample and quite what the plaque on the centre splasher represents I have no idea. The model can be supplied with smoke and steam and is DCC-enabled for those who use such stuff.

How good a current Hornby OO gauge A1 can look in a perfect surrounding is illustrated here on the Gresley Beat as it heads north, passing Mrs Wilberforce's street. Not many years ago, locomotives of this quality would have been the province of the supreme kit/scratch-builder. Not now.

Here's one of Hornby's earlier A1s running out of Welwyn North Tunnel's south portal on the OO gauge layout of that location built by Chris Worby. It's been modified and represents *St Simon* in very early BR days, still as an A1 and retaining right-hand drive.

Again on the Gresley Beat, this is one of Hornby's earlier tender-drive A1s, much worked on and substantially repainted (it might even have a proper loco drive). This was common practice in the past, where a reasonably accurate RTR body was exploited to make a half-decent loco. It's far less necessary these days.

When it comes to 2mm finescale, you've got to do a lot of work yourself when it comes to making locomotives, unlike the current OO range of locos where the hardest part in getting them to run is struggling to actually get them out of the ridiculous packaging. The late Dennis Brownlee was a master scratch-builder, as witnessed by this exquisite A1 heading the northbound 'Flying Scotsman' on the Model Railway Club's breath-taking Copenhagen Fields. The scene is just beneath where Mrs Wilberforce's house would have been and we're looking into the trough at Belle Isle as the Pacific is about to enter the southern portals of Copenhagen Tunnel.

Hardly a chapter this, more just a brief mention regarding the models available for this short-lived class. Despite delving into my photographic archive for hours, this is the only picture of a model Raven A2 I could find. It shows *City of Ripon*, the only Raven A2 to receive a Gresley A1 boiler and cab, and it's leaving the 'Cross on the Gainsborough Model Railway Society's massive depiction in O gauge of the LNER main line 'twixt London and Leeds. The loco is scratch-built. DJH made a Limited Edition kit for a Raven A2 in OO gauge (no longer available). I built one for a friend, though I took no pictures, and fitted an eight-wheeled Gresley tender to represent the loco later in its life. With the bigger tender, these 'Skittle Alleys' must have been the longest conventional steam locos in Britain (longer than a 'Princess Royal' or a P2?), though by all accounts they weren't that brilliant. I don't know of an O gauge kit for one, so the probable option is scratch-building.

Graham Farish have produced an N gauge A3 for many years, now with an improved Chinese-built mechanism courtesy of Bachmann, though the driving wheels are still way too small. The body is pretty basic as well, though it can serve as a decent starting point, particularly if the deficiencies are attended to. Just as in this case, the work of Paul Walker on his N gauge model of Kings Cross. Here, an ex-Farish A3 enters the terminus with the Up 'Talisman' and please note: even in this small scale, correct headlamps are carried.

Chapter 3
GRESLEY A3

Probably the most celebrated steam locomotive class of all time, and in *Flying Scotsman* we have arguably the most famous locomotive in the World. The type's popularity has resulted in dozens of modelling options down the years.

Starting in N gauge RTR there's the Graham Farish/Bachmann offering, and there might have been some early white-metal kits, though my knowledge of those (if any existed at all) is non-existent.

In OO gauge/4mm scale RTR, the first available model was the hideous Trix Twin *Scotsman*, so poor with regard to prototype fidelity that they omitted the definitive article. Useful only now to collectors, at a price to match, so rummage through long-forgotten cupboards and attics and, if you find one, quickly sell it and get something (or many things) that's right from Hornby. Next came the later Trix and Tr-iang OO A3s, both representing *Flying Scotsman*. The former looked better (though it didn't work – my oldest friend sent two back to Wrexham because of poor running and neither of

the replacements were right) but they put a corridor tender behind the BR version. Liliput then took on the Trix range, introducing tender drive in an effort to sort out the running.

At least Tri-ang put a non-corridor tender behind their BR one but it was the wrong sort (it should have been an ex-A4 streamlined non-corridor type, of which more later). Various Tri-ang/ Hornby versions then followed down the years, later ones employing tender drive but the combinations of loco/ tender were rarely right, particularly the GNR coal-rail tender which was way too fat in order to accommodate the tender drive. The latest Hornby A3s are brilliant in all combinations – they've even gone as far as to provide an A4-boilered version, complete with combustion chamber at the boiler/ firebox conjunction. For those on a tight budget, there's the cheaper Hornby 'Railroad' A3, which is less detailed but now employs the proper chassis, not the odious tender drive. It's an excellent starting point for super-detailing. For those who like a bit of real excitement there's also Hornby's live steam *Flying*

Scotsman set. For those who don't want to risk spoiling their Hornby or Bachmann A3 (or A1; Gresley and Peppercorn; and A4) models by messing up renumberings/renamings or weathering, TMC offer a quality service to do it for you.

The class has been well provided for in 4mm kits including (if my memory serves) Jamieson (as already mentioned, more of an A1), Wills, South Eastern Finecast, DJH and Finney. Some have been better than others and all have been rendered superfluous at a stroke (unless you like kit-building) by Hornby's RTR version.

In O gauge RTR we've had original Bassett Lowke (not really an A3 but if you like bent tin, then so what?), more recent Bassett Lowke and Ace Trains (carrying on the collectors' tradition) and finally the high-quality A3s out-of-the-box produced by both Bachmann and Sunset Models. DJH have produced kits in O gauge for A3s and also offer them as factory-finished. At the top end there's the Finney kit, and there might be others.

More on Cliff Parson's Gresley Beat in OO showing an A3 heading an A1, included to show the principal visual differences between the two types. The A3 is built from a DJH kit and the A1 a modified Hornby item. Note the superheater header covers on the smokebox of the A3 and the left-hand drive. The A1 has right-hand drive (note vacuum ejector pipe on side of boiler) but this is not exclusive to the lower pressure type, for as the original A1s were rebuilt to A3s they still retained their right-hand drive, some as late as BR days.

As a rule of thumb, though, all A1s had right-hand and all A3s built as such had left-hand drive. All had left-hand drive by the mid-'50s. Another point of interest: the A3 has a 'banjo' dome, something only fitted to the final 1934-built batch (2500-08), and this isn't one. If ever a detail feature on LNER Pacifics has caused so many inaccuracies in models (both RTR and kits), this has to be one of the most notorious. Dud drawings (Roche, Skinley and Beattie) have perpetuated the myth, as too have authors. So, in an attempt to put the

record straight – only nine LNER 4-6-2s ever carried 'banjo' dome covers, those A3s just mentioned, and then only until their first boiler change. No later Thompson/Peppercorn Pacifics had them (nor the V2s). What might have been underneath was a perforated steam collector but someone in the late-'30s/ early-'40s at 'Donny' (and there is no written record of this) must have decided it was easier to make a 'streamlined' dome cover with a straight taper in plan view rather than the 'peardrop' shape.

Above and below. One of Hornby's current A3s in the guise of the first German smoke deflector-fitted example, 60049 *Galtee More*. As already mentioned, such quality and accuracy has rendered kit-building in OO gauge of locos like this superfluous. However, even a model as good as this can be improved with just a little time and effort. Add on the bits supplied by Hornby, replace the bogie wheels (with Markits ones in this case), fit etched nameplates (247 Developments) and apply a dusting of weathering (though there can be too much of this).

Below. The prototype in question leaves Peterborough with an Up express on 7 August 1961, in a rather more scruffy appearance than my model. Photograph A.G. Forsyth, Initial Photographics.

Above. You can take things a step further by mixing and matching from Hornby. This combination of Thompson 94HP or 94A round-dome boiler and GNR-type tender is not offered by Hornby, so I just combined the two elements (and still had another A3 from the mixing) to make a model of the only pre-Grouping Pacific to survive *intact* into BR days.

Top right. Later in 1957, just back from its life on the ex-GC, *Sir Frederick Banbury* storms out of Kings Cross with a SO relief to 'The White Rose', the main train of which is alongside. Note the round dome-boiler on this A3.

Below. Things can be taken even further by carving off some of the moulded-on detail on Hornby's A3. There's the same amount of pipe runs on both sides of the smokebox of these models (the driven side should have less), so these were carved off on this loco and replaced with fusewire.

Bottom right. Just how good a current Hornby A3 can look in a layout setting is pictured here on Gilbert Barnatt's now-dismantled system. John Houlden has altered its identity to *Gladiateur* and covered it in a suitable coating of typical Tyneside grime.

Long before Hornby's latest A3 came along, my only way 30-odd years ago of getting a 'half-decent' model of a non-streamlined Gresley Pacific was to kit-build one. I thus built several Wills kits, chucked away (or didn't buy) the hopeless white-metal chassis and scratch-built my own. *Sandwich* is representative of this (there are others in this section) and, at close quarters like this, is showing its age, particularly with my less-than-sophisticated painting. In my defence, models such as this were not designed for close-up inspection – they're 'layout locos' (thanks to Iain Rice for the most appropriate description) and as such are expected to work in the knock-about environment of intense exhibition running. Running like this, on Wolverhampton MRC's layout of Charwelton, representing this ex-GC London Extension station before its final demise and closure.

Above and left. Another Wills kit, this time attached to a Jamieson tender. It represents *Doncaster,* one of a quartet of A3s fitted with the useless wing deflectors both sides of the chimney after there were complaints of drifting smoke after the locos received double chimneys. The other three were *Woolwinder, Pretty Polly* and *St Simon.* Why the little deflectors were fitted is a bit of a mystery, especially as their uselessness was fully understood before the war. They didn't last long and were replaced (with the exception of 60055) with the German trough type. Once again, its age and my less-than-perfect-painting condemns it to 'stand-off scale' (no nearer than three feet). However, in a layout context (in this case heading an Up car-carrier over Wolverhampton MRC's Stoke Summit) I hope observers accept that it looks all right. As for the red-backed nameplate, this is how Kings Cross Models used to supply them, even as a 'special order'.

With those small deflectors, 60112 *St Simon* runs north through Oakleigh Park on the down main, Sunday 10 July 1960. Photograph A.G. Forsyth, Initial Photographics.

Yet another Wills kit, this time representing the most famous non-streamlined Pacific in the World just at the time of its withdrawal by BR in January 1963 (as I'm writing this – January this year – I'm looking out over an identical Little Bytham winter railway landscape to that traversed by *Flying Scotsman* exactly 47 years ago on the occasion of her last run (below at Kings Cross) to Doncaster prior to preservation by Alan Pegler!). Correctly, she tows a streamlined non-corridor tender (one of only six tending to A1/A3 needs at any one time), ex-A4 (see why so many Flying Scotsman models have been incorrect down the years?) and this is a K's product from their P2, Bugatti-nosed kit. After withdrawal, 60103 exchanged tenders with *Lord Faringdon* to get a corridor sort, the problem for future modellers being that it was one of the trio with a cut-down back in order for the chosen A4s (*Mallard, Lord Faringdon* and *Seagull*) to be able to take water on the LM during the 1948 Exchanges. There'll be more regarding this modeller-confusing tender issue when I come to consider the A4s. And I should have put a speedometer on this model.

Photograph A.G. Forsyth, Initial Photographics.

Bassett Lowke also produces a late-BR version of *Flying Scotsman*, this one in coarse scale O gauge. It has a split smokebox door handrail (correct) and the valance is lined (correct), unlike mine but it, too, should have a speedo fitted (but does that matter in a model like this?). Note, however, that it does have (uniquely in the 'tinplate' market) the correct tender. There's more 'correct' Bassett Lowke stuff later, and I'll explain (immodestly) why!

South Eastern Finecast took over the old Wills range and re-introduced the model with a decent etched nickel silver chassis and the option of a GNR-style coal-rail tender. I built *Isinglass* in this guise, and she's seen heading out of Catesby Tunnel on Charwelton. Ian Rathbone's painting makes her look quite presentable.

A DJH A3 in OO gauge built by Steve Naylor. Problems with the pony truck's clearance has resulted in her running as a 4-6-0, though this is invisible when she operates on my layout. Steve built the loco as *Galtee More* and I renumbered and renamed her, adding weathering to complete this Tyneside-based A3. One thing I couldn't alter was the incorrect positioning of the vacuum exhaust pipe (it's too low) on the boiler side. I love this combination in A3s – GNR tender plus German-style smoke deflectors.

A DJH A3 in a layout setting, running past Eaton Wood on John Houlden's magnificent Gamston Bank layout in OO. Doesn't this look good, as *Minoru* heads southwards on an Up Pullman working?

Though John Houlden enjoys kit-building, he's not beyond exploiting what there is RTR, as shown by another modified Hornby A3 heading northwards through Gamston.

Though Hornby's earlier A3s were a bit dodgy mechanically, the basic body was well proportioned, and worthy of closer examination. This is just what Ray Flintoft did, and put a hand-built chassis underneath it, at the same time as tinkering with the body to produce another of the small deflector-fitted quartet, this time *Woolwinder*. It's seen on his Sowerby Bridge MPD layout.

In to O gauge now, and another one for the modern collector. This is Ace Train's coarse scale *Flying Scotsman* in first preserved guise, say the middle of 1963. It can't be in pre-war LNER days because it's an A3 (1947) and it's got left-hand drive (1954). Though it's got a corridor tender, it isn't the right sort (where's the beading?). Though one has to ask, do collectors care for accuracy? And it should have a streamlined dome - look at the prototype picture below.

Left. Another Ace *Flying Scotsman,* this time representing early BR days. It should still have right-hand drive and not have a corridor tender but I ask again, does it matter to this market? Lovers of bent tin are only after rarity – these are certainly not made of tinplate; in fact they're beautifully made with superb mechanisms, will go round switchback curves, haul huge trains and go fast. If that's what you want, well...

I'd better declare an interest here with regard to this current Bassett Lowke coarse scale O gauge *Flying Scotsman* because I was consulted by Terry Fox of Corgi (the then owners of BL – the whole lot's part of the Hornby brand now) before the model was made. The proving model in brass was brought to me after I'd provided much information. And look, it's got a streamlined non-corridor tender, correct for BR days. The twin tender version is also right. Not only do the tenders have beading but they're both cut down at the rear. Talk about collectors' stuff not being right. This Bassett Lowke A3 is more correct than umpteen so-called 'scale' models of *Flying Scotsman* I've seen down the years. Who'd have thought it?

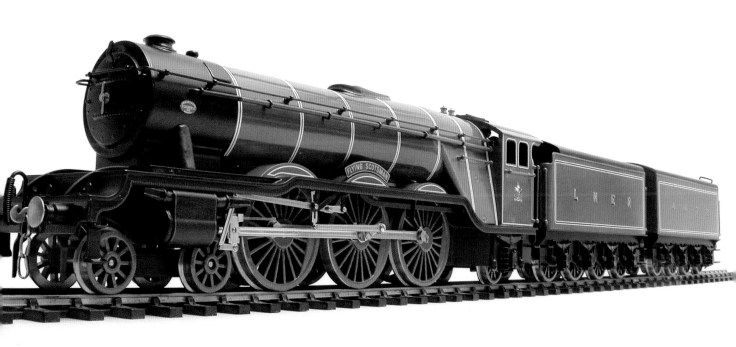

A different kind of RTR O gauge A3 is pictured here, on Mike Bisset's St Marnock loco shed layout. This is a Bachmann model, painted and weathered to perfection to represent one of the A3s sent to Holbeck in the early-'60s to work over the Settle & Carlisle and G&SWR metals between Leeds City and Glasgow St Enoch.

Sunset Models produced an O gauge A3 RTR a couple of years ago, and here's their LNER version on test on Pete Waterman's Leamington layout. The model represents *Flying Scotsman* in first preserved condition and, as such, should have a cut-down rear to its tender, making it less accurate in this respect than the Bassett Lowke version! It can be provided with DCC smoke and sound, and it certainly romped away on Pete's layout with a heavy load of Pullmans.

I took this picture of the Sunset BR *Flying Scotsman* at Telford some little time ago, and it's a pre-production sample. As such it shouldn't have green wheels or the firebox lined but the tender is correct.

Three views of DJH kit-built O gauge A3s running on John Ryan's Over Peover. These are splendid models made from splendid kits and if you want to build an accurate A3 in 7mm scale with as little grief as possible, then look no further than DJH.

Yet another *Flying Scotsman* model with two tenders, this time in O gauge finescale and again built from a DJH kit. The scene is on *British Railway Modelling* Editor John Emerson's Gifford Street Sidings and the loco is the property of Pete Marshall. I think these two tenders are correct, too. If making an O gauge A3 is beyond you, then DJH can supply one factory-finished.

If you have the ability and time, and you want to save yourself some money you can always scratch-build an A3 in O gauge (or any scale). That's what Barrie Walls does on his Wallsea and the results speak for themselves.

Middle and above. For those who strive for the highest possible accuracy in kits, then the Martin Finney product is probably the one to choose. I took these pictures of a completed Finney kit at Guildex in Telford some three years ago, though much to my shame I can't remember the builder's name. Perhaps if he sees this book he'll get in touch. From my own research I've concluded that *Robert The Devil* was the only A3 which kept its side handrails clipped to the smokebox ring after the German deflectors were fitted. All the others had theirs shortened.

Robert The Devil himself in mint nick, passing New Southgate on his (her?) way to town in May 1962. Note those superfluous handrails.

A Finney O gauge A3 in full flight. This is Mike Sant's work and it's crossing Hassell Harbour Bridge on the vast main line built by the Alsager Railway Association. Worthy of a close-up, glass case existence, isn't it still better to have magnificent locos like this hauling model trains, the like of which the prototypes were expected to pull?

Despite its chassis limitations (hopelessly small drivers and carrying wheels), in a layout setting the Farish A4 can look quite convincing, as illustrated here on Wilkersley Junction – a complete N gauge commission built by Norman Solomon.

Paul Walker has fitted the correct sized wheels to his Farish A4s for operation in and out of his Kings Cross, and the results are spectacularly different.

CHAPTER 4

GRESLEY A4

This must surely be the most celebrated class of all time, and the fact that this chapter is the longest is indicative of how popular these locos have been in model form. No fewer than six have been preserved (as a percentage of a 'numerous' class, that may be the highest, though so many Bulleids have been saved after years of mouldering away that I'm not sure). Three still run regularly today on our main lines and there are models available catering for this.

Hornby-Dublo was the first, pre-war, with their *Sir Nigel Gresley*, originally clockwork then three-rail electric. It was in LNER blue with full valances and is much sought after by collectors and, thus, extremely valuable. Post-war, the firm made several variations in BR livery; *Silver King* with single chimney (three-rail), *Mallard* with double chimney (three-rail) and *Golden Fleece* with double chimney (two-rail). After Wrenn acquired the tooling, myriads of different guises appeared, this time with a Tri-ang plastic tender to replace the naff bent-up tinplate affair (with coal lumps so huge, Hercules

would have needed to be the fireman!).

Trix made three or four A4s in two-rail OO, none of which had the right tender and, in my experience, ran very poorly, though the basic plastic body shell was very good (see later). They then became part of the Liliput brand and featured tender drive.

Bachmann then used that body and tender to produce a range of different A4s in OO, some of which are still current.

Hornby's first A4s (ex-Tri-ang, not Hornby-Dublo) in OO had tender drive and a dismal body moulding (all out of proportion) with armour-plated valve gear that often locked up as the tender struggled with a heavy load. That same body moulding has been used for their live steam set, which is a pity. However, the current Hornby A4 is fantastic – the best yet in 4mm scale – better than most kit-built examples. It looks superb and runs beautifully.

Kits in 4mm scale have included Wills, SE Finecast, Pro-scale and Martin Finney.

In the smaller scale we've had Lone Star OOO from the '50s – a push-along,

all die-cast affair of an A4 which some enthusiasts actually motorised. If they've stopped twitching yet is not known. Then there was the Minitrix A4 in N gauge, followed by the current Bachmann/Farish example. Langley (I think) used to make a rather lumpy cast-metal body and Foxhunter models made a superb white-metal kit, spoilt only by its need for a Farish A3 chassis. 'Decent' modellers made their own.

RTR O gauge A4s today have never been better. Years ago Cherry made a good RTR A4, and for collectors there's the Ace Trains examples. And now there are three outstanding Far East-made ranges of the streamliners, from Sunset, Golden Age and Lawrie Loveless.

There have been a few kits. Ace Models used the Ace Trains single-piece die-cast body for theirs, and the best O gauge A4 kits have been produced by DJH and Martin Finney. DJH can also offer an RTR A4, factory-built. The Right Price Loco Co has also produced an A4 kit in 7mm scale. Not so detailed perhaps, but a lot cheaper.

Tim Watson has taken the Farish body a stage further and fitted a scratch-built, 2mm finescale chassis for operation on the MRC's Copenhagen Fields. Here, one of the original quartet of silver A4s coasts through Belle Isle on the Up 'Silver Jubilee'.

Something for the beginners? Here we have Hornby's OO gauge *Spencer* from its 'Thomas' range, cheerfully hauling the Up 'Elizabethan' on my Little Bytham layout. It's passing a Wills A4 (of which more later). But don't knock *Spencer* too much. If it brings youngsters into the hobby, then so much the better, and look closely. That's Hornby's latest A4 underneath the nonsense and, though I haven't tried it, that daft face might easily come off!

Hornby's latest A4 is also available in the 'Railroad' range. The detail is simplified – there's no glazing, the valve gear is the older sort and it tows the original inaccurate tender. But the chassis has the five-pole, skew-wound motor and that loco body is spot on. So, if you want to save some money and you'd like to do some actual modelling, then start here.

Not content with just one or two A4s, Hornby often does Special Editions, like this model of *Merlin* in experimental BR violet (one of four). The attention to detail is incredible – note the 'incorrect' (though prototypically correct) curly-topped six on the cabside.

This is at the time of writing (early 2010) one Hornby's currently available A4 manifestations. It represents Gateshead's *Sparrow Hawk* just after the receipt of her double chimney. The body form is (at last!) spot on, attention to detail is incredible and the finish is superb. Note, too, the correct 'thin' streamlined non-corridor tender. Time was when manufacturers just lopped off the corridor connection from the rear and then told us it was now a non-corridor tender. Rubbish!

Despite the initial excellence, there's still room for improvement. What I've done here is add all the extra bits supplied by Hornby, fitted etched plates (247 Developments), changed the bogie wheels (Markits), closer coupled the loco to tender and handed it over to John Houlden for weathering (Tyneside-based A4s were only clean after shopping).

Sparrow Hawk before being modified is seen alongside a full-blown Hornby make-over. This has all my mods applied, plus a complete repaint by Ian Rathbone. Note how Hornby's rendition of BR green is a little too 'blue'.

Another modified Hornby A4 in a layout setting, this time as *Quicksilver* heading the Up 'Tees-Tyne Pullman' on Gilbert Barnatt's erstwhile OO gauge ER main line.

What a 'fiddled with' Hornby A4 can look like in a layout setting is seen here as my *Dwight D Eisenhower* rests on shed on the late Frank Dyers's Borchester Market.

Hornby A4s are justifiably popular with modellers, to the extent in John Houlden's case that he's replaced all his previous kit-built examples for operation over Gamston Bank. In this view, *Seagull* heads the Down 'Yorkshire Pullman'. John altered the tender to make the cut-down back example appropriate for 60033.

Left. When I was trainspotting at Doncaster/Bawtry/Retford in the summer of 1960, *Gannet* (and *Merlin* from Haymarket) were always on 'The Elizabethan', to the extent that we'd have liked another one or two. So, since my 'Elizabethan' is representative of that period I had to have her, courtesy of Hornby with just the few mods already described. I've an idea, though, that the nameplate should be red-backed (as in the prototype picture below, taken a year later) as she races through Little Bytham 50 years ago.

Bachmann make an OO gauge A4 as well, though it's not a patch on Hornby's. This is their *Quicksilver* (though not quite original – the Cartazzi truck has been modified). The tender is wrong for 60015 (she only towed a 1928 corridor type for a few months in 1960 and the electric warning flashes put the date as 1961 or later). The split chassis is now obsolete.

Still, time was when the Bachmann A4 was far superior to Hornby's and when it was first released in the mid-'90s (as 60009) I thought I'd have a go and see what could be done. Here's the result. I scratch-built the back end frames, replaced the bogie, lowered the front numberplate, thinned down the valve gear, chucked away the ghastly corridor tender and built a replacement Crownline tender. I added the strip at the tender tank base to make it correct for 60002 (there were two other non-corridor tenders with this ex-'Coronation' feature – those towed by 60001 and the smashed-to-bits-in-the-war *Sir Ralph Wedgwood*, later attached to Class A2/1, *Highland Chieftain*). Ian Rathbone did the complete repaint.

The real thing shortly after receipt of her double chimney in 1957 but before the fitting of the electric warning flashes. 60002 was one of the last A4s to get these (60011 never did) and the pushed-back position of the nameplates meant there was space to put the front ones higher up (unlike most others). Note, as well, that flange on the tender.

Above. I did much the same sort of thing with another Bachmann A4, this time making a Wills corridor tender, cutting down the rear end to suit. Then, a few years later the grotty split chassis fell to bits. Not wanting to waste Ian Rathbone's superlative painting, I made a complete SE Finecast chassis for her. The results (and performance) speak for themselves.

Left. In 1955, the real thing rests on Haymarket after 'Elizabethan' duty. The cut-down rear of the tender is clearly visible.

Trix (Liliput) provided the basic body shell for the Bachmann A4 and, as mentioned, it's basically right. Right enough for Roy Jackson to use on his epic recreation of Retford in EM. Here's one on a scratch-built chassis on 36E. The front numberplate could do with lowering slightly.

I had Hornby-Dublo A4s in my younger years but was never satisfied with the chassis or tenders. So, in an effort to 'improve' things I scratch-built chassis for them and made Wills tenders to be towed. Complete repaints and renumberings were undertaken as well, and here's one of the results. Finer handrails made a difference, too, though the complete thing was pretty crude.

Left. The Hornby-Dublo 'learning curves' were subsequently sold and the building of Wills kits was undertaken. Scratch-built chassis were employed rather than the white-metal lump suggested. I painted *Silver Link* to begin with, later stripping it down in disgust and handing it to Ian Rathbone to do a proper job.

Below. 60014 *Silver Link* with an up express at Potters Bar on 16 July 1960. Photograph A.G. Forsyth, Initial Photographics.

Though not as 'crisp' as Hornby's RTR A4, in a layout setting the Wills A4 certainly looks at home, as epitomised by this shot of 60014 topping Stoke Summit on the Up 'Anglo-Scottish Car Carrier'.

I built many SE Finecast A4s for customers during my time as a professional model maker. Successor to the Wills range, at least they feature a proper etched chassis. Just to keep my hand in, I built a couple for myself, including *Miles Beevor* (the last A4 I 'copped', though I didn't see them all). She's (he's?) seen here romping through Little Bytham on a Down parcels train. Correctly, she tows a non-corridor tender, by courtesy of Crownline.

Left. In rather more shabby condition than my model, *Miles Beevor* has just run through Oakleigh Park, right at the end of GN steam in 1963. My loco's on a similar duty. Photograph A.G. Forsyth, Initial Photographics.

For the more brave amongst us, a really top-grade A4 in 4mm scale could be obtained by building a Pro-Scale kit. But it needed some making. Good friend Mick Peabody started two (to represent *Mallard* and the one seen here, *Kingfisher* from Haymarke~). He got the chassis running but gave up with the complex bodies, handing them over to me to complete, ready for Ian Rathbone to paint the pair. I think they turned out all right, though judge for yourself as one of 64B's finest prepares for the 100 mph dash down to Peterborough as she takes the Up 'Elizabethan' over Stoke Summit in the summer of 1961.

O gauge RTR A4s are now numerous in number and choice. We start off with Sunset's model of *Silver Fox* in almost original condition (the buffers are full length, the drawgear is not recessed and she has front numerals). The tender is right, representing as it does an original 1935-built type complete with bow-ended rear to match the streamlined stock. However, this being a pre-production sample, the stainless steel fox on the offside is running backwards and the inspection hatches in the valance should not all be open.

Sunset's representation of *Mallard* in the condition she was in when she broke the world speed record for steam traction. Available with DCC sound and smoke, this is a fine model, though one would have thought in a model of this quality the lubricator drive off the offside rear crankpin should have been included.

The Loveless RTR A4 in O gauge in the guise of *Silver Fox* - a higher quality model than the Sunset version indeed.

Loveless also supply an A4 in the general-purpose green guise.

Bottom left, left and below. The stainless steel-adorned 'Coronation' A4 from Loveless is particularly attractive, even down to the Canadian bell and coat of arms for 4489. Correctly, she tows a second hand 1928, ex A1/A3 corridor tender.

The real thing at Top Shed.

The Loveless version of *Mallard* in record-breaking guise.

Middle and left. In BR green the LL O gauge A4s look stunning (this is how I remember them), and all have opening cod's mouths and smokebox doors. *Silver Link* even has the unique style of firebox handrail (where it dipped down only after the penultimate stanchion – all the others dipped down after the one before), though in single chimney guise she should not have electric warning flashes.

Right. The Loveless A4s do have the lubricator drive present.

Above and right. Current day A4s are also represented in the LL range.

Though not truly 'historically' correct (in BR blue 60007 should have a single chimney), this is how the prototype looks now, complete with commemorative post-war speed record plaque on its flanks, as represented by the Loveless A4. So, if you want to run A4s alongside Class 66 diesels, this is the way to do it.

The other top quality producer of RTR A4s in O gauge is Golden Age Models, like the Lawrie Loveless examples, factory-finished in Korea. The range is just as extensive and they run superbly, and are also DCC enabled.

Left. The Golden Age A4s also feature an opening cod's mouth and smokebox door.

Below. And, if you want a present day *Sir Nigel Gresley,* then Golden Age can supply one, though it really should have the commemorative plaque on the cladding sides.

Above. *Bittern* in present day state is present in the range, too, complete with incorrect corridor tender (historically, she never towed a corridor type). I believe the tank is brand new after her recent restoration. That being the case, why was yet another 1928 corridor tender top produced, with old-fashioned beading (60007, 60009 and 60010 also has one)? Why was the opportunity not taken of putting a 'proper' A4 corridor tender behind her – a 1935, streamlined corridor type?

Both below. But it's on a layout that the Golden Age A4s really shine, where their prodigious hauling powers can be put to the test. And John Ryan's Over Peover presents a perfect stamping ground – over 100' long with the opportunity of seeing full-length trains. *Dominion of Canada* has charge of the 'Yorkshire Pullman' (Golden Age's own cars) and *Empire of India* the 'Flying Scotsman' (Golden Age's carriages). Both are in full 'Coronation' regalia.

The manufacturer considers it sacrilege to weather a Golden Age A4, but John Ryan thinks they look better (I agree). In these shots, all is not quite what it seems, for *Mallard* could be portrayed as about to smash the record on July 3rd, 1938 – there's the dynamometer car and shortened streamline set, but look closely. She's carrying the commemorative plaque on her sides, something not fitted until after the war.

Time was when the only way to get a 7mm A4 (or any other Gresley Pacific) was to scratch-build, which is what the Gainsborough Model Railway Society did for their amazing rendition of the main line between Kings Cross and Leeds.

DJH's kit for a 7mm A4 will usually turn out well if the builder's any good. Here's *Mallard* in BR guise, created from just that source.

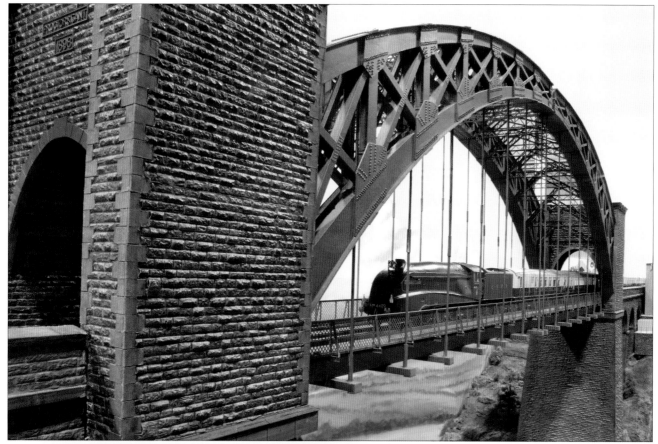

Top left. I suppose the Finney A4 kit is the top of the tree in the 7mm kit stakes for an A4, though some solderers (like me) dislike a resin boiler. Whatever, the results can be outstanding, as shown by this early BR rendition of *Gannet* running on Holiday Haunts. But, where are its lamps?

Above and left. More Finney excellence, this time running over Hassell Harbour Bridge on the Alsager Society's extensive (and extremely impressive) O gauge FS system.

CHAPTER 5
GRESLEY P2 and THOMPSON A2/2

If ever a class of locomotives is bound to stir controversy, it's Thompson's A2/2s. Rebuilt from Gresley's magnificent (though flawed) Mikados, one would have to try particularly hard to create a MORE ungainly locomotive than appeared from Doncaster in 1943. I've included model pictures of the P2s in this chapter, just to illustrate the amazing difference and to complete the story. How Thompson got away with such a costly (and useless) rebuilding during the dark days of the Second World Was has never been fully explained, but the result was that post-war spotters were denied the sight of arguably the most majestic British locos of all time; instead we got some oddities scrambling about on secondary duties between London and Newcastle.

The first model P2 (as *Cock O' The North*) was made by Marklin in coarse O before the war, but that's hardly a modelling option unless you're super-rich, and it's pretty crude.

K's did kits for *Earl Marischal* and the 'Bugatti-nosed' four in OO gauge, and Pro-scale did the same for *Cock O' The North*. Millholme Models also did a hand-made, limited production run of the prototype in OO gauge. If there are O gauge kits for P2s then my ignorance precludes me from mentioning them. Lawrie Loveless does a quite brilliant 7mm finescale version RTR.

As for the A2/2s, such is their 'popularity' that they'll never be offered RTR, in any scale, though there have been a few kits. There was Millholme's grotty affair and there's DJH's excellent example in 4mm. There's also the DJH 7mm kit, also available factory-finished for those who have the money though not the time and/or skill.

All three photographs above and opposite. As mentioned, for O gauge modellers, the P2 is available RTR from Lawrie Loveless, here in the guise of *Cock O' The North* in original condition. It has all the usual features.

Above and left. In the author's opinion, this was the supreme manifestation of the P2, also available from LL. Wherever one's allegiance lies, no other British steam loco ever looked as impressive as this. Thompson will surely never be forgiven. The class of six should have been transferred to the ECML during the hostilities where their prodigious strength would have been invaluable. Haymarket shedmaster, Mr Lund reckons that any perceived problems with the giants on their indigenous road could be laid squarely at Cowlairs' poor workmanship (not their fault, but the biggest thing they were used to before was a Reid Atlantic) and union intransigence (Dundee's insistence on having two meant that half the time they burned coal just to cover the firebars as they languished on shed between duties). As for spreading the track, a far less costly solution (never considered by Thompson) would have been to alter the front pony/leading driver arrangment to link the two. That way, we would have seen them unsullied and at least one would have been preserved. If only Sir Nigel had lived a year or two longer!

Below. Lord President in the flesh.

A comparison of the two Loveless front ends. Eventually 2001 (and 2002) were rebuilt to have the conventional streamlined nose. Then, disaster!

Seen on the Gresley Beat, this is Cliff Parson's scratch-built original P2 in OO gauge.

More scratch-building, this time to create what *Cock O' The North* became. Can you believe it? This A2/2 is by Barrie Walls in O gauge and she rests between duties on Wallsea shed. She still retains the original (shortened) P2 boiler. Later on she, and 60502/5/6 would receive replacement Thompson or Peppercorn A2/3/A1/A2 boilers.

A DJH A2/2 kit-built in O gauge. Strictly speaking, the side handrails should be clipped to the front of the smokebox. Such are the joys of 'engine picking'.

Left. In the mid-'70s I was considering making models of the Thompson oddities, though lacked the courage to scratch-build in OO (or any gauge). I thus commissioned Mike Edge to make a model of 60506. In fairness, he was learning his trade as well and the model (although quite well made) had many inaccuracies. It still had an original boiler but also a cut-back cab (only appropriate to the re-boilered quartet). The chassis also needed a bit of work to get it working to my satisfaction. Eventually I rebuilt it to conform to what I really wanted, and got Ian Rathbone to paint her. The appearance of DJH's A2/2 meant this one was sold on. She's seen in the days when she was my property, running up to Stoke Summit.

Middle. More of my part scratch-building in OO gauge to create one of the A2/2s that retained its original boiler (one fewer cladding band) and full 'V'-fronted cab retained. The tender, cab and firebox came from K's own P2 (this was my take on the rebuilding) and the rest was made from brass. Jamieson supplied the valve gear. I no longer own this model. I painted it and it's a bit too clean for one of New England's allocation.

A Millholme A2/2, though should I say that part of this is from a Millholme kit? The chassis is modified (Millholme's valve gear cannot be built as supplied in my opinion) and the firebox has been lengthened, the cab altered to make it correct and a proper dome substituted (yes, it came with a banjo dome). The model represents *Thane of Fife*, the only one to carry a Thompson Diagram 117 boiler; note the streamlined dome on second ring, even though there was a round steam collector underneath. The tender is scratch-built (Millholme's was a hopeless mess with both rivets and beading – rivets on an A2/2 tender?). It's running on Leighford, Wolverhampton MRC's erstwhile enormous OO gauge creation. DJH's 4mm A2/2 rendered the Millholme version obsolete, but then, it always was! I built and painted this model and no longer own it.

Two A2/2s from my current OO collection. 60501 has a Peppercorn Dia. 118 boiler and 60504 retains its original. Note the difference in the cladding bands and the shape of the cab front. *Cock O' The North* was the prototype for DJH's kit and *Mons Meg* is built from a Crownline kit. Ian Rathbone painted them.

The real *Mons Meg*, with a lipped chimney, pauses at the platform end at Kings Cross before crossing to the station loco yard on February 21st 1960. Photograph David Idle, www.transporttreasury.co.uk

Cock O' The North runs under a bridge on Charwelton – there is a precedent for this since York's Pacifics were regular visitors to the GC, at least as far as Woodford Halse, 60501 included. 60501 and 60502 had beaded tenders, the other four having streamlined non-corridor examples.

My current *Wolf of Badenoch* (I've built at least four models of this loco). It's from a DJH kit, painted by Ian Rathbone and is seen hauling an Up parcels past Stoke Summit's solitary 'box.

Right. A Nu-Cast A2/1 running on Roy Jackson's Retford in EM (passing a much more illustrious relative). Obviously it's *Duke of Rothesay,* because that's the only one that would be regularly seen; by me as well, for this is the place where I used to watch LNER Pacifics.

Below. Here's my Jamieson hand-cut kit-built A2/1 running on Little Bytham on a fitted freight, a typical working for this singular New England-based member of the quartet. I ordered the bits from EAMES in 1976 for *Duke of Rothesay,* specifying an eight-wheeled tender. No luck, I was given a six-wheeled one, only appropriate for the class in its early days. I originally fitted a Wills A2 tender (too fat, beading and no rivets – quite wrong, even for an A2!) and she's now got an SE Finecast A2 tender – quite right this time. I painted her and at 34 years old I still own her. That's the loco's age, not mine.

Bottom right. A Nu-Cast A2/1 in the guise of Haymarket's *Robert The Bruce.* She's on a running-in turn on Stoke Summit and is as supplied, other than the hopeless cast-metal lump of a chassis having been chucked out and replaced by a scratch-built one in brass. Ian Rathbone painted her.

CHAPTER 6
THOMPSON A2/1

Not much of a model selection here for there aren't many available. If there are any 7mm kits available I don't know of them and the choice in 4mm is very limited – Jamieson hand-cut (if you can still get one), Nu-Cast (now Autocom) and PDK (ex-Crownline). The choice for those who model in 2mm scale is non-existent, and I don't know of any RTR A2/1s in any scale.

Right. Yet another Nu-Cast A2/1, this time running on Eric Kidd's OO Scottish Region-based layout. It's *Highland Chieftain,* the one with the flush-sided tender inherited from the smashed up A4 from the Baedeker air raid at York during the war (it should really have a steel strip attached to the tender's sole plate, an inheritance from its 'Coronation' days). 60507 is passing *Humorist* – the only A3 to have full-sized smoke deflectors.

Below. 60507 in early BR days (it still has a rimmed chimney), ready to go at Waverley. You can just make out the steel strip at the base of the tender's tank.

Below right. I built this Crownline kit for a customer a decade ago and Ian Rathbone painted it for me in the form of *Waverley*, in early BR condition but still in apple green livery. That completes the whole class, though like 60510 (and 60507), her presence on Stoke Summit would only be after a Doncaster Works visit.

Shortly after I commissioned Mike Edge to scratch-build me an A2/2, I asked him to scratch-build an A2/3. There were similar problems with this one, and I ended up making a new boiler for it. The tender (which, in fairness, Mike didn't supply) is from a Wills A2 with the beading removed, but it should have rivets. Prior to selling this model, I fitted a Crownline riveted tender, painted and weathered it.

A Millholme A2/3, made up by me (and painted by me) running on Leighford. I say Millholme, though the chassis is scratch-built with Jamieson valve gear, the firebox has been lengthened and the tender has been narrowed, the beading taken off and the turned-in front removed. You see, the firm foolishly used the Skinley drawing as a guide. If ever you come across these kits on second-hand stalls, leave well alone! Unless they're free – in which case the thick metal makes excellent ballast once it's pounded up or melted down!

CHAPTER 7
THOMPSON A2/3

A few more kits have been available for this type, Thompson's most successful Pacific design. In 4mm we've had Millholme, Crownline and DJH and in 7mm DJH. Though usually kept away from top-link jobs, the A2/3s were very powerful and were well regarded by their crews. Just think, if Edward Thompson had not rebuilt the P2s, not rebuilt *Great Northern* and only produced a few new Pacifics, he'd have been remembered with great affection for designing the B1s – a great mixed-traffic design. But he did, and he isn't!

Here we have a Crownline kit for an A2/3, built and finished by Norman Venus in OO gauge. It's seen on Billingham, the prototype-based layout from the Middlesbrough club.

And yet another DJH A2/3 built in OO gauge, this one completed by John Houlden and running on Gamston Bank. *Ocean Swell* still has her original Thompson boiler with round dome on the second ring, again something easily catered for in the kit.

And here we have a DJH A2/3 in OO, built and finished by Ray Flintoft. It's fitted with a Peppercorn boiler, something catered for in this excellent kit.

Two of my Ian Rathbone-painted A2/3s are shown here. *Edward Thompson* is built from a Crownline kit and represents the loco still with its original boiler cladding and rimmed chimney. Later, like all the others, she'll get a Peppercorn boiler and lipped chimney (though 60514 and 60519 retained their ugly chimneys to the end). *Hycilla* (what a lovely name for a filly!) also retains her original boiler cladding (it has one more section than 60500 and 60511 for a short time) and rimmed chimney. The other A2/3 we run, *Dante,* has the streamlined dome and lipped chimney. I really should have drilled out 60516's chimney, though why DJH don't cast it hollow I don't know.

A DJH kit-built A2/3 in O gauge, romping around the outdoor section on John Ryan's Over Peover. As with all other DJH 7mm locos, a factory-finished one is available.

When John Houlden wanted an A1/1, he didn't scratch-build it, but made it up from bits from a DJH A3 kit, the result being excellent I have to say.

Though I have little love for Thompson's big work (he prevented me from seeing a P2!), I build models of what I saw, and *Great Northern* was a daily visitor to Retford during my spotting days. Thus, at the time (33 years ago), with no kit anywhere near, I scratch-built one in OO gauge, and the result is seen here. Misguidedly, I used the Roche drawing and got a few bits wrong (Isinglass, where were you when I needed you?). I'll let the reader pick them out. I painted it and, as with many of my earlier efforts, it is no longer is in my possession.

CHAPTER 8

THOMPSON A1/1

I never thought there'd ever be a kit for this particular loco, but Crownline did one in 4mm scale, and it's now available from PDK. Yet another controversial rebuilding by the master's successor, many consider it sacrilege that Gresley's pioneer Pacific should have been so horribly altered. Actually, in truth the original *Great*

Northern was quietly dismantled in Doncaster works and all the bits used as spares (apart from the wheel centres, some sundry pieces and the tender which were used on the new loco). An almost brand new loco thus emerged. Though it could be argued that Thompson's A1/1 was more powerful than the A10 it replaced, it wasn't

anywhere near as good as a double-chimney A3 (which it would have become if the tinkering Thompson hadn't fiddled about). As it was, the sole example of this unhappy piece of railway history operated on secondary duties from Grantham or Doncaster shed throughout its BR life until it was put out of its misery in 1962.

John now builds professionally and this is an A1/1 from one of his commissions, as seen running on his OO gauge Gamston Bank. Actually, it was an over-run commission of mine, and I handed it over to John to build it for me for my customer, who was delighted with the result.

This is my current *Great Northern*, built from a Crownline kit, painted by Ian Rathbone and running on my Little Bytham layout. Far superior to my previous scratch-built effort, you can see why I sold the former.

Great Northern backs out from Kings Cross; short-lived Sulzer Type 2s have ousted the traditional 0-6-2Ts.

The best model of the rebuilt *Great Northern* I've ever seen – scratch-built as a Scale 7 commission by Steve Barnfield. I know this book tries to consider overall modelling options, but if you want a model of this quality, then it'll cost you. You never know – perhaps even more than pieces of ancient bent tin!

Left. O gauge is always easier to photograph than anything smaller, particularly if you're after realism. Mind you, good (or exceptional in this case) modelling is needed, and you won't see anything better than this – Bob Merry's scratch-built *Scottish Union.* It's running on Holiday Haunts and is passing another example of Bob's work in the unmistakeable shape of an A4. Both locos were painted by Alan Brackenborough.

Below. Another scratch-built A1 in O gauge, also painted by Alan Brackenborough. This is the work of Barrie Walls and it's hauling a Pullman rake on the outdoor section of his Wallsea main. Might this be the Digswell Viaduct at Welwyn? Don't worry if the thought of scratch-building an O gauge A1 is beyond you, or even kit-building one, for DJH can supply one factory-finished, and they do look good. It's just that both Bob and Barrie (who are good friends) prefer to scratch-build.

For OO gauge modellers, the release of Bachmann's A1 some years ago was a real boon, until folk tried to run them hauling prototype-loads, and the motors burnt out! There was a blanket recall and the chassis was rejigged to take a Mashima motor. The result - beautiful running. This year Bachmann are to introduce the A1 in the form of *Tornado* itself, complete with modified tender (the real thing has more water capacity than the BR ones). This is their mock-up from 2009. It should prove to be a winner.

CHAPTER 9
PEPPERCORN A1

Though jumping slightly ahead in the chronology, it makes sense to consider the A1s ahead of the A2s (even if the A2/2s have appeared before the A2/1s in this book). In N gauge we've had the Foxhunter kit for the A1 and in RTR OO we have the Bachmann model. Kit-wise in 4mm we've seen examples from DJH, Pro-Scale and Crownline.

In O gauge you can obtain an A1 RTR from DJH or you can kit build one from the same source (if you can get it, for it was a limited edition). Other kits have been available in 7mm from David Andrews, Ace Models and (I think) The Right Price Model Co.

Not a bad selection to represent arguably the most successful Class 8P locomotive to grace our rails. I say successful in the widest sense – by the time you add up initial costs, maintenance and the miles run between overhauls without failure, the A1 comes out by miles the most economical big loco. And they could pull a house down, assuming the crew could hang on! A travesty that one was not preserved, at least we can now enjoy the sight and sound of a brand-new A1 in the marvellous form of *Tornado*. And with regard to *Tornado's* appearance on the main line, I've included as a final chapter to this book a complete article from *British Railway Modelling* where I built a model of her in OO gauge from a DJH kit to be auctioned off, all proceeds going to the A1 Trust. It raised £2,200! I also built another A1 for myself at the same time.

The Bachmann A1 has been available, and still is, in both guises; Doncaster-built with prominent rivets and Darlington-built with (invisible) countersunk rivets. Examples of both types are illustrated here. *Meg Merrilies* represents an early BR green example with rimmed chimney, high front numberplate and first BR totem. *King's Courier* is much later, even to the extent of having a split smokebox door handrail and lowered top lamp bracket. It should, therefore, have electric warning flashes.

Despite it being a fine model out of the box, there's still scope for improvement for those who still prefer to 'do' things. The nearer A1 has had etched-brass deflectors fitted (spares from a DJH A2/2 or A2/3 kit) and better bogie wheels put on. It's also been renumbered, renamed and weathered. More has also been done, as will be explained in the next picture.

Even though the Bachmann A1 has had its motor problems sorted out, it's still too light on its feet for my needs, and without more ballast, a heavy express freight such as this topping Stoke Summit would cause much slipping. My *Scottish Union* has lead in just about every spare space under the bonnet and the spring on the bogie has been discarded. She's also had the rear footplate raised to match the tender sole plate (see how the two unmodified A1 rear footplates are lower than the tenders). The 'thin' deflectors also show up well in this three-quarter front shot.

In the days before RTR A1s and even complete kits in 4mm scale you either had to scratch-build or modify. But modify what? Wills had made an A2 for donkeys years (it was designed around a Tri-ang Britannia chassis, of which more later) which is a sort of A1 with smaller drivers and a shorter smokebox. So, I built four A1s from this source. The mods consist of a scratch-built chassis, longer smokebox (turned from copper central heating pipe – in my teaching years I had access to a complete, comprehensive school metal workshop; the only thing I miss!) and a scratch-built centre footplate, complete with miniscule splashers. The lack of rivets meant you could only really make a Darlington-built example. It's running on Biggleswade and the painting is my work. I keep it for sentimental reasons – the other three have long gone.

Then along came the DJH A1 kit – a revelation indeed. At the time (the mid-1970s) it was outstanding with its mix of appropriate materials for the job. It still is. Here are five of mine (I've built umpteen more), arranged to show the variations that delight engine pickers. Rivets or not, dome position, electric lighting retained or not and livery variations. All of these have been painted by Ian Rathbone.

The shots on these pages show three of my A1s in layout action, all hauling Pullman trains – a regular occurrence for an A1, and certainly on the 'Yorkshire Pullman' or 'Queen of Scots'. *Bongrace* heads 'The Harrogate Sunday Pullman' on my Little Bytham layout, *Kestrel* does the same over Stoke Summit (I don't have a headboard for this train!) and *Hal O' The Wynd* takes the longest distance Pullman working past Westby, just south of Stoke. Though reasonably detailed, all my Pacifics (and all my other engines) are 'layout locos', made to work with the odd dent now and then. Anyway, I don't think they are quite good enough for a closely looked-at, glass case existence. But they do 'go', as I hope many of my customers will testify.

John Houlden has also built umpteen DJH A1s, and he paints his. East Ranford was his previous exhibition layout.

When it comes to models that have to work hard to earn their keep, the locos Roy Jackson builds for his EM Retford are second to none. *Sea Eagle* just needs lamps to complete the realism on this scene looking south across the flat crossing. It, too, is made from a DJH kit.

Golden Age Models is to introduce an O gauge A1 RTR this year. This is the test model and the Korean craftsmen obviously don't know about how the roller bearing A1s had only one lubricator, had circular keeps to their external axleboxes and had snap-head rivets. But this is a 'proving' model and the production ones will be dead right. I sent a large heap of notes to the proprietor, so if it isn't right, blame me!

When *Tornado* first ran on the Great Central it was in shop grey (TMC commissioned Bachmann to produce a run of models in that guise). I took my model *Tornado* along and popped her on the footplate to take this shot. Is the real thing ONLY 76 times bigger?

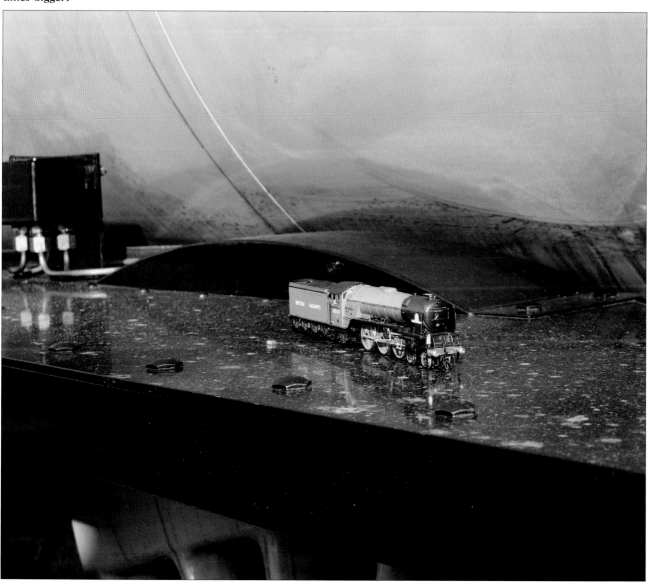

Left. In my days of innocence, I built a Wills A2 and fitted it onto a Tri-ang Britannia chassis, fitting Jamieson valve gear at the same time (I'm a 'scale' modeller remember?). I cheerfully put the alternator in the wrong place, fixed on the banjo dome and made the over-wide tender, complete with its beading. It was what was supplied and the instructions said so. Mr Roche, you have a lot to answer for! And here it is, whizzing past on Fordley Park in the days when I was young. They're Hornby-Dublo Pullman cars as well – even then, my modelling standards were low!

Below. *Blue Peter* in the same style as my model (other than not having its motion) ready for repair at Doncaster. The numberplate is on the top hinge strap and the cross-rail is still in one piece. Latterly, her top lamp bracket will be lowered and the cross-rail will be divided.

CHAPTER 10
PEPPERCORN A2

The last Pacific design to be built by the LNER (though only the first one), the A2s (and the A1s) I suppose took the best of Gresley's ideas and the best of Thompson's, and brought the two together. So we had long connecting rods, divided drive, separate sets of valve gear and a good chassis. The result, like the A1s is extremely handsome.

Model-wise, Trix made an OO gauge version in the late-1960s, but the chassis was grotesque (though it worked well) and it had a corridor tender. It also had a banjo dome! Wills made a cast-metal A2 years ago, as mentioned, designed to go on a Tri-ang 'Britannia' chassis. It was pretty naff, for the Roche drawing was used, of which more later. SE Finecast tidied it up and the result now is a decent kit, but DJH's is the best (in my opinion) 4mm kit for an A2. Crownline did one (OK if you like a resin boiler – I don't; it stinks when you try to solder it!). PDK might reintroduce it.

In O gauge we've had the DJH kit (and their factory-finished one) and there might be others. As I've said, you'll have to forgive my ignorance, though a glance at the adverts in the Gauge O Guild *Gazette* should help. Finally, Golden Age Models will introduce an O gauge RTR A2 this year. Bachmann are to introduce an OO gauge A2 later this year.

Left. I still have that old Wills A2, but it's been altered a bit. It's now got the correct dome and a proper tender (DJH), the chassis now has brakes and weathering and I've repainted it, though the alternator is still in the wrong place (too well soldered on). She stands in front of a much better A2, made up from a DJH kit and painted by Ian Rathbone (it featured in the Right Track series of railway modelling DVDs, Parts 1, 2 and 3). Both A2s have double chimneys but *Blue Peter* has the multiple valve regulator arrangement as well. This was fudged up from odd bits and pieces.

60539 BRONZINO running light from Edinburgh back to Tweedmouth on 30 May 1962. Photograph Michael Mensing.

Another (distant) Retford view as a DJH A2 heads south on a running-in turn. Take a look – it has a single chimney; a rare Scottish-based example and an instant 'cop'. It's Roy Jackson's work in EM.

Bachmann are producing an A2 in RTR OO gauge this year, and this is one of the test models. It'll be available in several manifestations – single or double chimney, liveries, etc, and it looks very good. Unlike its sister A1, it'll have etched-brass deflectors.

Bottom left and above. Before Bachmann announced its A2, Graeme King set about converting one of their A1s (they are, after all, very similar). He shortened the chassis, altered the wheel centres and fitted B1 wheels, altering the rods and gear to suit. He wrote about it in *BRM*. I think he's mad, but the results speak for themselves.

Bottom left. Graeme's mad enough to embark on another A2 conversion, this time to make one of the multiple valve regulator locos, *Sugar Palm* from York. Seriously, this to me is what railway modelling used to be about. Railway modellers actually modelling! Such is the excellence of today's RTR offerings that we're in danger of becoming lazy, just mere purchasers.

Left. A DJH A2 kit made up in O gauge, seen on the turntable of John Ryan's Over Peover. You can get one like this factory-finished from the same firm.

Below. Golden Age Models are to introduce an RTR A2 in O gauge this year, and this is the 'proving' model. Models of this quality cost a fair bit (around two grand) but they are outstanding and do represent wonderful value for money. Having said we're becoming lazy, it would still be rather nice to own one like this, and then use the spare time to do some layout work!

CHAPTER 11
GRESLEY W1

A singular loco to say the least, and one not totally ignored by the kit makers. In fact, it's two very different locos (both inwardly and externally), and the following pictures show it in both guises. I have to say (unlike the P2-A2/2 rebuilding), the rebuilt loco looks the better – not so porcine. That said, the original looked impressive. Way too young to have seen the original (I was minus nine when it disappeared), we only knew the W1 as the 'un-named Streak'.

In 4mm scale we've had the SE Finecast kit for both versions and Dean Sidings produces a one-piece resin casting for the rebuilt version to fit on a modified Hornby chassis. In O gauge there's the Ace kit for the original and DJH for the rebuilt version.

The original W1 in battleship grey livery heads underneath the North London line on The Gresley Beat in OO. This is made from a SE Finecast kit with the tender flange removed for accuracy with the regard to the corridor tender. Remember, the corridor tenders were full width and the kit gives you an over-wide soleplate – an inheritance from the Wills days.

This page and overleaf. Here we have the W1 in original condition in O gauge. It's the work of Nick Dunhill and he's made it from an Ace kit, or should I say 'started' using an Ace kit, for there's precious little left unaltered of what was supplied. Nick's one of the up and coming generation of loco builders and his work is as good already as anything I've photographed by the 'masters' – Beeson, Miller, Green, Reynalds, etc. He also does his own painting.

105

Top and middle. The rebuilt W1 in O gauge, made from a DJH kit and, like many others in this book, seen on Over Peover – thanks John. This is in BR guise but it can be supplied with full valances and the option of a corridor tender.

Below. The W1 at Carr Loco, Doncaster, on September 5th 1954. Photograph A.R. Carpenter, www.transporttreasury.co.uk

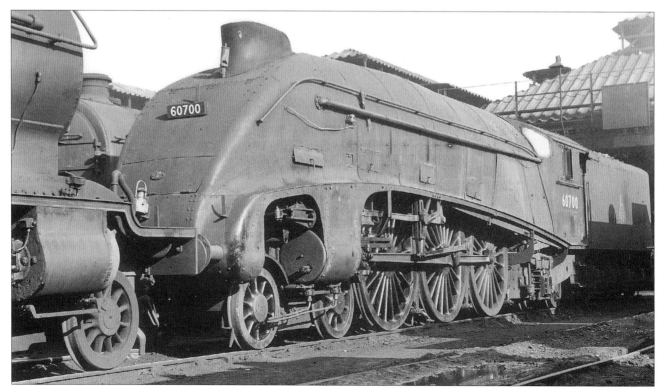

John Houlden's W1 running up Gamston bank. Like mine, built from a SE Finecast kit, his is much dirtier (and more realistic?). He does his own painting – it would be sacrilege to ruin Ian's painting with heavy weathering.

My SE Finecast W1 as running on Stoke Summit in OO. I asked Dave Ellis for one of his A2 tenders, swopped for the one supplied. The original's too fat (corridor tender width), and I just filed off the rivets on the A2 tender. The painting is the work of Ian Rathbone.

Though most of the models in all the chapters are historic, in that they represent locos from the past, some of the prototypes are still very much alive and kicking. Thus, if you want to run your Loveless or Golden Age 60007 A4 in blue on a layout that represents the current scene, then here's your proof. On 21 June 2008, *Sir Nigel Gresley* approaches Sleaford on 'The Cathedrals Express' from Lincoln, bringing back memories of Sunday diversions. On 28 November 2009, though, she was on her own main line, sweeping south through Little Bytham on 'The Tynesider'.

CHAPTER 12
CURRENT PROTOTYPES

Another up-to-date A4 on its main line in the form of *Bittern* heading 'The Brighton Belle' through Careby on 25 July 2009. This, too, is available in its current guise from Lawrie Loveless or Golden Age.

Here's *Tornado* in action on the main line for which the original prototypes were designed. She's powering north near Creeton, on 23 May 2009, heading 'The Cathedrals Express' for York.

CHAPTER 13

Some kitty-nitty-gritty; this final chapter is taken complete from the October 2008 edition of *British Railway Modelling*. It shows how the magazine conducts in-depth reviews of products, and that the finished results can be seen at exhibitions. **OF COURSE THE TORNADO BID OFFER IS NOW LONG GONE** and defunct so no bids please – but – it reminds you of what you might have missed! For full details of *BRM*, please visit the website www.brmodelling.co.uk

FAST STEEDS indeed

To coincide with the completion of *Tornado*, **Tony Wright** builds a pair of DJH A1s in OO gauge. Prototype photographs as credited,

At some point between its construction (10/'49) and its naming and repainting to BR green (7/'52), the eventual *Great Central* reverses out of King's Cross and heads for passenger loco or Top Shed. In BR blue from new, the loco still has its rimmed double chimney and has (obviously) earlier brought in the 'Tees-Tyne Pullman'. This was one of the five roller bearing ones. **Paul Chancellor collection**.

Long ago, in the mists of time (April, 1994), a lad named Tony Geary wrote an article for *BRM* describing how he built a DJH A1 kit in OO gauge. That loco, 60114 *WP Allen*, is still doing yeoman service on Stoke Summit (indeed, it'll be running at our Peterborough show, October 18 and 19). At the end of Tony's piece there was a description, by Mark Allatt, Chairman of the A1 Steam Locomotive Trust, of how a brand new full-scale A1 was to be built, of which more later.

So, why another article on building an A1 from the DJH kit, and not just one, but two? It's over 18 years since Tony Geary's A1 article appeared in the April, 1994 edition of *BRM*, and that's long out of print and unavailable. My methods of construction are different in many ways from Tony's and, one hopes, several

newcomers to kit-building have emerged in this new century. Finally, and the most important reason for presenting this account, in 2008 we should see a brand new, twelve inches to the foot scale A1 running in Great Britain, 60 years after the first one appeared on the newly-Nationalised railways. Obviously, one of the A1s I build will represent *Tornado*, and the other, *Bongrace*, hopefully to show the visual differences between the two siblings, born (or perhaps that should be completed) 60 years apart. And the reason for building one of these kits as 60163? The A1 Steam Locomotive Trust is to be congratulated on the most astonishing achievement in building the 50th member of this wonderfully reliable and economical class. By way of supporting the Trust, this model of *Tornado* is to be the subject of a sealed-bid auction at our

forthcoming Peterborough show, or by post, the highest bidder securing the model, with all proceeds given then to the A1 Trust. As mentioned, the model will be built from a DJH kit to professional standards (I used to build locos professionally), guaranteed for my remaining lifetime, painted by Ian Rathbone and be as accurate (given the 'constraints' of the kit) as possible. I hope the blokes who own the 20+ DJH A1s I've built down the years will testify to the model's potential 'quality' (as with all the other ex-LNER 'big stuff' it's been my pleasure to put together in the last quarter century for customers world wide). Full details of how to 'bid' as it were will be found at the end of this article. And *Bongrace*? I'll keep that to run on Little Bytham - you can't have too many A1s for a latter day ECML steam depiction

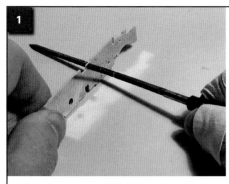

1 The top hat bearings provided were the 'thick-walled' variety, and the holes in the frames needed opening out considerably. The two red marks on the broach indicate the difference in diameter between the two. Needless to say, I used the 'thin-walled', and wore sticking plaster to begin with *before* blisters appeared!

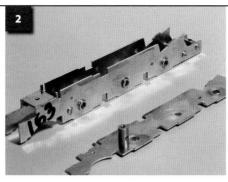

2 Such is the accuracy of DJH's frame etches that no jig was necessary to ensure alignment. After the bearings were soldered into position, the three turned spacers were fixed onto one frame, the opposite side located and then the flat spacers soldered in place.

3 Brake hangers and shoes were soldered in place before the wheels went on, giving this impression of a galley from antiquity. Double-sided PCB strips for pick-ups were soldered onto the cross-members. The frames were painted at this stage, behind the driving wheels.

4 Wheels on (Markits' latest LNER pattern), pick-ups installed and coupling rods attached. The brake shoes have been bent down into place and everything checked so that no binding/shorting takes place. Watch *Right Tracks* 1 & 2 to see how I arrange this in motion.

5 The prime mover chosen was the usual, excellent combination of Mashima motor and DJH gearbox - in this case a GB1, ready-assembled. Running-in was, also as usual, accomplished by using the Bachrus 'Saddle', frequently mentioned in these pages.

6 As supplied, the DJH A1 cab cannot be folded up to produce the subtle rake-in between the base of the side windows and the top - metal won't bend in three directions at once. I ran a piercing saw along the rake-in line, bent up, and filled the resulting gap with solder.

7 Both cabs folded and ready to be installed on the footplate. *Bongrace's* (right) has prominent rivets (Doncaster-build) and *Tornado's* has a flush appearance (most appropriately, Darlington-build). The rake-in to the tops is clearly evident.

8 A fair bit of work is needed on the main castings in preparation for soldering everything together. This was the progress to date at the Glasgow show last February where the models formed part of my display. *Bongrace* (top) has her bits held together with friction.

9 The prominent central feed nibs on the footplate's centre and offside have been carefully removed and cleaned up. The boiler bottom has to have more metal removed to accommodate the porcine motor (this kit was designed around open-framed motors).

10 At the Glasgow show (on the sound advice of Tim Shackleton) I was introduced to this 400 grit 'mesh', available from Sigeberht Magna Railways (Michael & Nora Sharp). What a fantastic product - ideal for 'finishing' white metal, and it never clogs.

11 Although, in the main, the fit of DJH's castings is excellent, occasionally a bit of filling is necessary. The backward 'dip' on the firebox top is crucial for getting the 'look' of an A1 dead right. Too many kit-built A1s fail in this, their fireboxes looking dead straight on the top.

12 Low-melt solder was the chosen medium for filling, introduced from the rear, holding the work so that gravity assisted. Again, this technique is fully explained in *Right Tracks* 1 and 2, where I build (among others) a DJH A2 which has exactly the same firebox.

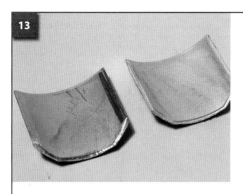

13 By raking in the cab, you'll find that the cab roof is then too wide. Mr Geary and Mr Cockcroft suggest cutting the cab roof at the rainstrips and taking half a mil' or so out. I filed off the internal lip so that the cab roof sat flush on the sides.

14 I concede that the cab roof is still a bit wide (even after filing the eaves back a bit). The cab is designed to be bolted to the footplate - this always leaves unslightly gaps (see Frank Dyer's very first review of this kit in *Model Railways*) and is better soldered in place.

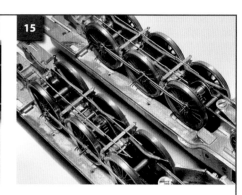

15 When I installed *Tornado's* motor/gearbox on the centre axle, it was slightly noisy going forward (the Law of Sod epitomised), so I fooled it by turning it round and driving off the rear axle. Success, and she was then just as quiet in reverse. I left well alone after that!

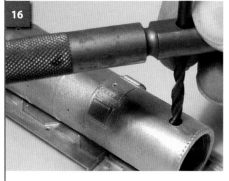

16 If I had a criticism of DJH's big 4mm locos it's that they never provide 'hollow' chimneys. I can understand the ease by which solid castings can be produced, but the following pictures show the difficulties facing the builder. First, open out the hole in the smokebox.

17 In the past, I've glued on such chimneys with epoxy, leaving them plugged and only taking pictures from low angles. If you try to drill out glued-on chimneys they shear off, often getting wrecked in the process. So, soldering in place becomes obligatory.

18 Soldering on is best accomplished from the inside, and definitely not in one go. Tack, check, and, if adjustment is necessary, unsolder and 'wiggle' into the right place. Expect burnt fingertips! When you're happy, drill a couple of pilot holes dead centre in each pot.

19 Don't try and drill the full diameter in one shot. I'm always cautious wnen using a mini drill in this way - bad experience in the glued-on days when the chimney broke free and the bit gouged into the top of the smokebox. I said 'Oh Dear' a few times!

20 Always make sure your bits are sharp (blunt drills can actually melt low-melt solder with the friction they create) and get close to what you want using just a bit in a tap wrench. Don't try and rush this process, for the consequences are dire.

21 The final opening out of the apertures can be achieved by using a tapered cutting broach, with a 'healthy' blob of spit as a lubricant - apply by each finger in turn to stay healthy and safe. Ingesting bits of white metal, however much lead-free, is not healthy!

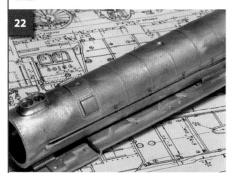

22 Throughout all aspects of the build, information was gleaned from the late John Edgson's Isinglass drawing of the class. I cannot stress how valuable such accurate drawings are for plotting positions for items such as the blower pipe, here fixed on the driver's side.

23 The whole of the front end - frames/footplate/steps/ bufferbeam - is made up from etched parts, and I think the etching masters are a bit old by now, for some of the slots were a bit 'blind' and certainly the fit was very tight at times.

24 Like the cab, I think the front assembly is designed to be screwed/bolted on - not good practice in my opinion. As usual, I soldered everything together - more secure and no gaps. The slot for the front coupling was cut *before* the bufferbeam was soldered in place.

can you? Especially as 60128, under Grantham's 'Curly' Royce's command, achieved the highest power output by a member of the class, charging over Stoke Summit and topping 90 mph in record time, with a full weight train behind the tender! Truly, in terms of day-to-day reliability and performance, the A1s were unsurpassed.

Research

For building the BR-condition A1, the usual RCTS, Ian Allan and Irwell works were consulted, along with the scrutinising of countless photographs - jobs I've done countless times. For the first-hand research into *Tornado*, I'd like to offer my most grateful thanks to Mark Allatt, David Elliott, Bob Alderman and all those guys actually building her for their help, provision of drawings and hospitality when Richard Wilson and I popped up to Darlington in April to see and photograph the actual thing.

Construction

I remember visiting DJH's shop when they were based in Banbury, shortly after their A1 kit first appeared, nearly 30 years ago now. Back then, it was justifiably deemed to be 'revolutionary' with its mix of etched-brass/nickel silver and highest-quality white metal castings. It was indeed, and today still is, in my opinion, one of the finest loco kits on the market. In the main, it's supplied as a Doncaster-built example, with prominent snap-head rivets. However, for those who want a Darlington-built example, flush-sided cabs and

tender bodies can be supplied by DJH.

Granted, as designed the DJH A1 kit is really 'just' for OO modellers, though with a bit of work it can be built in EM without difficulty, even in P4 if your name's John Cockcroft.

As is customary now, the sequence of pictures show how I got on with building this brace of A1s.

How to bid

If I were building *Tornado* on commission today, it would cost over £1,000 - inclusive of materials, my time and Ian Rathbone's painting. Bearing this in mind, a minimum starting bid of £650.00 is expected. To make your bid *via* post, please send it to Tony Wright at the Editorial address, clearly marking the envelope A1 Trust Bid. Please

Tornado, still part-finished at its home in Darlington last April. By the time you read this, she should have completed trials on the GC with a view to main line running this autumn.

During its last major overhaul, 60117 *Bois Roussel* is seen partly dismantled in the Crimpsall at Doncaster 'Plant'. The smokebox appears to have been patched-repaired and the asbestos sealing ring will need attention before the smokebox door is re-instated. Judging by the lack of conduit on the fireman's side of the firebox, she's lost her electric lighting, though the supporting bracket at the top of the smokebox is still in place. As modellers, we often struggle to ensure the boiler-side handrails are horizontal, true and straight. I occasionally wonder, why? **Paul Chancellor collection**.

25 The Stone's generator was soldered in place before the right-hand deflector was shaped up and the rails added, and it was fixed on. A length of 5 Amp fusewire forms the conduit to the top lamp. Try to make the deflector handrails line up with the boiler ones.

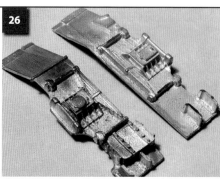

26 *Tornado* has Timken roller bearings all round (five of the BR-built A1s had, too), resulting in a circular end to the axlebox keeps on the Cartazzi frames and the tender. I soldered on a small brass washer to create this effect. She also has a battery box each side.

27 Both front ends completed to show the differences. *Tornado* (right) should have a more pointed front to its generator. The extra pipes are for air brakes and steam heating, and, I'm told, she'll be fitted with an AWS bang plate. Sprung buffers are from Markits.

29 Judging by the eccentric on the nearside rear crankpin, I assume 60163 will have the Smith-Stone type of speedometer, latterly fitted to most, if not all, the BR-build A1s. I just made one up from a crankpin washer and vacuum standpipe, bent to suit.

30 *Bongrace* was one of the A1s fitted with a Flaman speedometer when new, though there's little evidence it was ever used. The bracket remained for at least a decade after the drive was removed, and I just fashioned it from scrap etch laid over the Isinglass drawing.

31 The new A1 has some subtle changes from the originals. Because of lower height restrictions the safety valves are shorter (cut-down Markits) and the whistle is on the fireman's side (ex-*Kestrel* I believe). The whistle itself was fudged from some spare brass castings.

32 Both complete apart from from the motion. *Tornado* will have hers fitted *after* Ian Rathbone has painted them. The new A1 is slightly lower overall, with squatter chimney, dome, safety valves and cab roof. I filed a little off these items, though it's hard to tell.

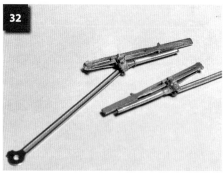

33 Crossheads, slidebars and connecting rods. I have to say, this part (and the rest of the valve gear) of any loco's construction is a real fag. DJH's motion is typical in that the crosshead slipper (in white metal) won't fit the slidebars as supplied - much filing being necessary!

33 Some of the castings were showing the age of the moulds by now, including the cylinders. A fair bit of cleaning up was necessary, particularly where the stub ends of the slidebars and piston rods were to be fitted - essential for friction-free running.

34 I always split valve gear assembly into both halves when finishing off a chassis. As is well known by now, I never use rivets for assembling valve gear, preferring brass pins and solder. It was *much* easier for Ian to line the wheels *before* the gear was on.

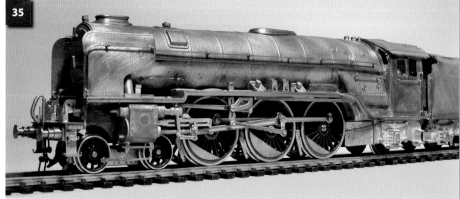

35 *Bongrace* complete prior to going off to Ian for painting. Little in the way of cleaning has taken place - I leave that to the painter, though he complains I use too many fibreglass refills and they're the very devil to shift, only truly appearing after priming.

LEFT: When I first saw *Bongrace*, I was ignorant of the French connection and prounounced her name to my urchin chums with the second syllable as in 'ace', little realising that it should be the same as in the slang term for one's posterior. Again, she's beatifully painted by Ian, and, I have to say, in the livery I prefer.

on Stoke Summit over the weekend. The deadline for the sealed bids is 4.00 pm on Sunday October 19, an hour before the Festival closes. The plan is then to open the bids, and the highest bidder presented (if present) with the locomotive on the *BRM* stand. So, if you think your bid will be successful, then make sure you're at the show on the Sunday afternoon. A member of the A1 Steam Locomotive Trust will be present. If there is more than one top bid, then lots will be drawn. All proceeds will then go to the A1 Steam Locomotive Trust.

This is a unique opportunity to acquire a professionally-built and painted OO FS locomotive. It has a definite provenance, and is signed by the builder. In time, its value might well increase.

Happy bidding!

FAR LEFT: I fitted a crew of three (at least) in *Tornado's* cab, courtesy of Springside, though shouldn't the figures be wearing bright orange overalls? Detail shots like this show the quality of Ian's paintwork - just admire that thin red lining around the frames. Yes, I know Bachmann's A1 has probably rendered the kit-building of such handsome locos superfluous, but a decent kit has a crispness and 'one-off' quality that only one made by hand can possess, especially with as good a paint job present on this pair.

Above: *Bongrace* in the condition I've modelled her - 1956/'57. She still has the original BR totem but her front numberplate has been moved down to the top hingestrap. She's heading an express near Stevenage and has just gone under the famous 'Ha'penny' footbridge. An interesting feature is the leading carriage's roof splashed with water, caused by 60128's picking up water at Langley. It's a feature I've never seen modelled. **The Transport Treasury**.

include your full name and postal address, and telephone number/email address as well for preference. Alternatively, you can leave your sealed bid at the *BRM* stand during the *National Festival of Model Railways*, at Peterborough over the weekend of October 18 and 19 next. The model will be displayed on the *BRM* stand during the show, with the occasional run

LEFT: Both locos 'faces' capture very well that familiar Doncaster/Darlington style. *Bongrace* has Markits' latest correct 12.2 mm LNER Pacific bogie wheel, but for *Tornado* I opted for the standard 12mm type - extra clearance and all that. I know the (fairly generous) curves my own locos will have to negotiate, but *Tornado* - who knows? Pragmatism?

1 DJH's outside frames for the tender are a bit old-fashioned in that they retain the (prototypical) outside-bearing facility. A sub-frame is the preferred method (a Mr Geary modification), though I'm happy with just opening out the bearing holes with a mini drill.

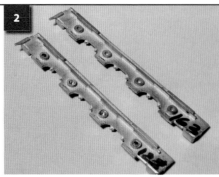

2 The drill I used is a perfect fit for squeezing in Peco 'cup' brass bearings, the fit being so good that friction holds them in place. Only the first and final axles require these bearings - the centre axles just go along for the ride, giving any necessary side play.

3 The curve to the tender tops is pre-formed for you by DJH, and the bodies just needed forming along the half-etched lines. The sole plate is secured to the frames by 8BA screws, fitting into the soldered-in white metal securing pads.

4 *Tornado's* wheels are spoked (not uncommon on A1s) - these are easier to make than discs. Obviously, no water scoop apparatus is fitted to the new A1's tender, and she has a well-tank too, something I haven't modelled - it's invisible from normal viewing angles.

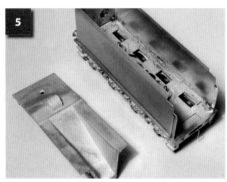

5 With the tender body soldered on to the sole plate, attention can be turned to fixing in the coal space. Items such as rear steps and rear handrails must be affixed *before* the casting is soldered in place, thus ensuring, as it should be, soldering is internal.

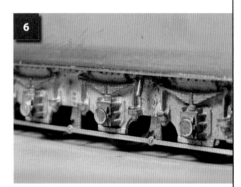

6 As mentioned, on the new-build A1 all journals have roller bearings, represented here (as on the Cartazzi frames) by small brass washers. They should have A1 TIMKEN cast on them. 60163 also has two water feed pipes, one each side, for bowser replenishment.

Tornado after returning from Ian Rathbone's paintshop. The quality of his workmanship speaks for itself - he even hand-painted the RAF coats of arms. Nameplates are beautifully etched by 247 Developments. The model was finished by early July, so some assumptions as to 60163's final (first) appearance had to be made. This, I'm told, is the condition she'll be in when fully painted at York later this year, after proving trials on the Great Central. The word is that the prototype will eventually be in BR blue, then BR green. I can't wait.

7 *Bongrace* had plain bearings, as represented by the DJH kit. The five A1s built by BR fitted with roller bearings were incredibly economical in terms of their mileage between shopping, soon repaying the extra cost of the items.

8 *Tornado's* tender will have a lot more on than a BR A1. As well as the normal hoses there's a pair of air-brake pipes and an ex-coach alternator, complete with a protection plate. The location points are partly supposition, it not being completed at my visit.

9 The major difference between the two locos' tenders is the increased water capacity of the new-build. The coal division plate is further forward (reducing the coal capacity) and the area around the tank filler is built up to be flush with the sides.

10 60163's tender complete, on some of the drawings supplied by the Trust. I cut down the tank filler to be almost flush. The tender front is different (obviously no water pick-up lever) and there might well be further boxes to add - the builders weren't quite sure!

USEFUL CONTACTS

British Railway Modelling, Warners Group Publications, West Street, Bourne, Lincs PE10 9PH. www.brmodelling.co.uk

Ace Trains: www.acetrains.com

Ace Trains Owners Club: www.acetrainsownersclub.org.uk

Ace Products: P.O. Box 700, Reigate RH2 7YF. Tel. 01737 248540

Autocom UK: Tel.01264 332323

Bachmann/Graham Farish: www.bachmann.co.uk

Bassett-Lowke Society: www.bassettlowkesociety.org.uk

David Andrews: Tel. 01242672744. www.locomotivekits.com

Dean Sidings: P.O. Box 68, Lydney, Glos GL15 6WW

DJH: Consett Business Park, Villa Real, Consett DH8 6BP. Tel. 01207 500050

Golden Age Models: Tel: 01929 480210. www.goldenagemodels.net

Hornby/Bassett-Lowke: www.hornby.com

Hornby Railway Collectors' Association: www.hrca.net

Isinglass Drawings: www.isinglass-models.co.uk

Ian Rathbone: Tel. 01214453610

John Houlden: Website: www.whistlestoprailways.co.uk

Langley Models: Tel. 01293 516329. www.langleymodels.co.uk

L H Loveless & Co: Tel. 01423 712446. www.cockothenorth.net

PDK Kits: Tel.01209 860551. www.pdkmodels.co.uk

Martin Finney Kits: 1 Poolestown Cottages, Thornhill, Sturminster Newton DT10 2SQ. Tel. 01963 362400

Sunset Models: Unit 24, Redhouse Industrial Units, Rectory Road, Bacton, Suffolk IP14 4SB. Tel. 01449 781010

South Eastern Finecast: Glenn House, Hartfield Road, Forest Row, East Sussex RH18 5DZ. Tel. 01342 824711

TMC: Tel. 01947 896040

Tri-ang Society: www.tri-angsociety.co.uk

Trix Twin Railway Collectors' Association: wwwttrca.co.uk

Wessex Pro-Scale: Units 1 and 2, Silverhills Buildings, Decoy Industrial Estate, Newton Abbot TQ12 5LZ. Tel. 01626 363301

Wrenn Collectors Club: www.gandr-wrenn.co.uk